HAMPSHIRE & THE NEW FOREST PUB WALKS

Ruth Paley

COUNTRYSIDE BOOKS
NEWBURY BERKSHIRE

First published 2019

Reprinted 2021

COUNTRYSIDE BOOKS
3 Catherine Road
Newbury, Berkshire

To view our complete range of books,
please visit us at
www.countrysidebooks.co.uk

ISBN 978 1 84674 388 7

All materials used in the manufacture of this book carry FSC certification

Photographs taken by Ruth Paley

Produced through The Letterworks Ltd., Reading
Designed and Typeset by KT Designs, St Helens
Printed by Holywell Press, Oxford

CONTENTS

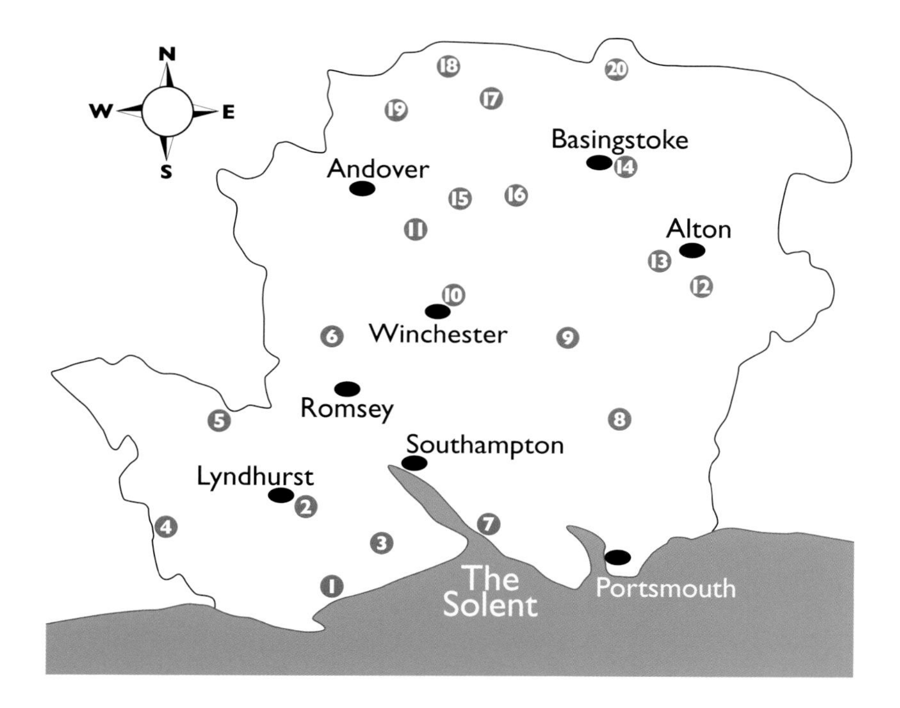

PUBLISHER'S NOTE

We hope that you obtain considerable enjoyment from this book; great care has been taken in its preparation. Although at the time of publication all routes followed public rights of way or permitted paths, diversion orders can be made and permissions withdrawn.

We cannot, of course, be held responsible for such diversion orders and any inaccuracies in the text which result from these or any other changes to the routes, nor any damage which might result from walkers trespassing on private property. We are anxious though that all the details covering the walks are kept up to date and would therefore welcome information from readers which would be relevant to future editions.

The simple sketch maps that accompany the walks in this book are based on notes made by the author whilst checking out the routes on the ground. They are designed to show you how to reach the start, to point out the main features of the overall circuit and they contain a progression of numbers that relate to the paragraphs of the text.

However, for the benefit of a proper map, we do recommend that you purchase the relevant Ordnance Survey sheet covering your walk. The Ordnance Survey maps are widely available, especially through booksellers and local newsagents.

INTRODUCTION

A village pub, preferably with perilously low beams, a roaring log fire and a couple of scruffy dogs asleep under the tables, is as much a part of an English village as the cricket green and red phone box. As post offices and village shops close, the pub is also playing an increasingly important role in community cohesion, providing a central point for local people to come together and share a bonding moan over the state of the nation with a pint of real ale.

These walks all start at or pass a pub so please visit each and every one as you walk. Pubs are closing at an alarming rate and put simply it is a case of use them or lose them – for once a pub is gone it is normally gone for ever.

The Hampshire countryside is a delight for walkers, stretching from the South Downs National Park in the east to the New Forest National Park in the west and the North Wessex Downs in the north. With rolling hills, chalk streams and thatched cottages, these pub walks explore the charm and natural beauty of Hampshire's different landscapes, national parks and stunning coastline.

Each walk gives details on distance and parking – which is mainly in pub car parks so please check with the landlord if the pub is open, avoid parking over busy periods and most definitely visit the pub at the beginning or end of the walk. The introductions include advice on whether there are hills, stiles and its suitability for dog walkers, as well as where you might find sheep – or New Forest ponies! There are ponies everywhere in the New Forest, standing in the middle of the road, waiting in pub car parks, or wandering down the village high street. There is a forest byelaw that forbids you from feeding them and as they are not tame, it's best to walk round them and not try to stroke them. A 'Place of Interest Nearby' section at the end of each walk offers a relaxing way to finish off your day, suggesting National Trust houses, museums, or historically significant landscapes.

I hope you enjoy exploring the wonderful county of Hampshire, and its many delightful pubs, just as much as I have enjoyed putting together this selection of walks, and I wish you many days of sunshine and successful walking.

Ruth Paley

Walk 1
Keyhaven Marshes

Distance: 4 miles (6.4 km)

Map: OS Explorer OL22 New Forest. **Grid ref:** SZ306914

How to get there: Keyhaven Marshes are on the coast just east of Milford on Sea and 5 miles from Lymington. Follow Lymore Lane, then Keyhaven Road to the Gun Inn and the car park. **Sat nav:** SO41 0TP.

Parking: Pay and display car park opposite the pub. Bring change as it costs more to pay by card.

This level walk follows the Solent Way by the salt marshes with wonderful sea views towards Hurst Spit, Hurst Castle, and the lighthouse, as well as the Needles and the Isle of Wight. From medieval times until the 19th century this area was home to the salt industry. Now, these atmospheric salt marshes are home to many ground-nesting birds, with dogs allowed on the seawall path, but not on the reserve. After following the coast, the second half of the walk cuts inland across the reserve to return to Keyhaven. This is an intertidal mudflat and salt marsh so for safety stick to the paths, where you can enjoy the views across the marshes. It's a wonderful place for a walk all year round, with the ponds, ditches and lagoons home to arriving migrants in spring, including swallows and chattering flocks of little terns, while overwintering brent geese, wigeon and pintail seek refuge in the colder months.

THE PUB

THE GUN INN is a quirky 18th-century pub with carved crab tables and nets strung across the ceiling. There are tables at the front by the road and a large beer garden at the back. It is often busy with a queue for food, as the saltmarshes are popular with walkers. Children are only allowed in the beer garden so if you are looking for something more family-friendly an alternative option is the **Smugglers Inn**, 1.5 miles away in the centre of Milford on Sea. This friendly pub serves food every day from 12 noon to 9.30 pm, with log fires and a children's play area in the garden. It's also dog friendly.
The Gun Inn (no website) ☎ 01590 642391
Smugglers Inn 🌐 pubsnewforest.co.uk ☎ 01590 644414

The Walk

1. Go through the small pedestrian exit at the top of the car park to the start of the harbour wall. Now walk with the wall on your right until you come to a small gate on your right. Go through

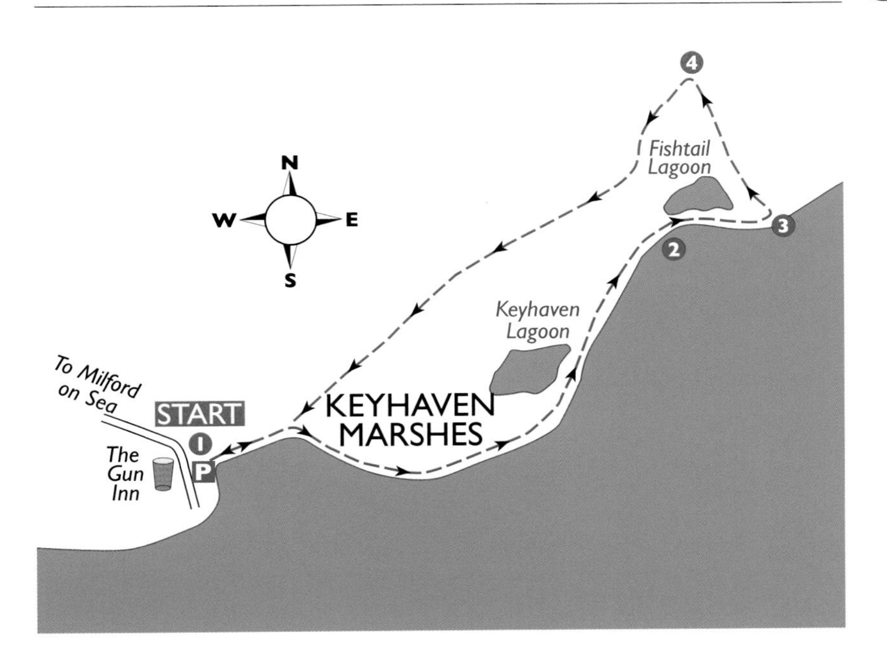

the gate, passing an information panel, and follow the gravel path with wonderful views across the harbour on your right and **Keyhaven Marshes** on your left. The sea turns to salt marshes and is a haven for waterbirds. Pass **Keyhaven Lagoon**, then when you see **Fishtail Lagoon** on your left, there is also a choice of path.

2 Either drop down to the gate and information panel and continue along the lower path, or stay on the higher path with views across the sea. Both routes will take you in the same direction. Ignore a path on your left down steps, and stay on the main path until you come to a jetty.

3 Now you leave the sea and turn left to follow a wide gravel track, taking the upper path when the route splits. Walk inland until you come to a gate and small parking area.

4 Go through the gate and turn left, following the path by a former landfill site that has now been landscaped into a lake. Ignore side turns and continue on until you come to a gate. Walk by the side of

the gate to join a single track road and you will soon find yourself back by the harbour wall and the mouth of **Avon Water**.

Place of Interest Nearby

Hurst Castle sits impressively at the end of a 1½ mile coastal spit. Built by Henry VIII, it was once one of the most advanced artillery fortresses in England, built to guard the Needles Passage, leading to the Solent, the port of Southampton and the important growing naval base at Portsmouth. It now offers panoramic views across the Solent towards the Isle of Wight and is managed by English Heritage. To get there, you have the choice of walking along the shingle spit from the beach at Milford, or catching a ferry from Keyhaven.
🌐 hurstcastle.co.uk/ferries

Walk 2

LYNDHURST

Distance: 5 miles (8 km)

Map: OS Explorer OL22 New Forest. **Grid ref:** SU296087

How to get there: The Waterloo Arms is ½ mile north of Lyndhurst centre, on Pikes Hill, off the A337. **Sat nav:** SO43 7AS.

Parking: The Waterloo Arms has a large car park and are happy for customers to leave their cars while they walk. If you aren't planning on using the pub, there's a small forestry commission car park at the eastern edge of the village, at point 2 of the walk.

This is a wonderful walk in the heart of the New Forest. Close up views of the lovely shaggy ponies are guaranteed, as well as open heath, shady woods and a chance to explore Lyndhurst. This bustling village has been known as the capital of the New Forest since it was chosen by William the Conqueror to be his royal hunting ground, in 1079. Famous former residents include Alice Liddell, the inspiration for Lewis Carroll's *Alice's Adventures in Wonderland,* who spent most of her life here. Her ashes are buried in the church of St Michael and All Angels where there is a memorial plaque to her.

THE PUB

THE WATERLOO ARMS is a traditional 17th-century inn with a large and welcoming beer garden. Food is served all day from 12 noon, with dogs and children welcome, it's also reasonably priced. Although you have a five-minute walk from the pub into the centre of Lyndhurst, the roads can get very congested so another definite advantage of this pub is that it keeps you away from town centre traffic jams.

waterlooarmsnewforest.co.uk ☎ 02380 282113

The Walk

1. From the **Waterloo Arms**, turn right and follow **Pikes Hill** to the main road, then right again into **Lyndhurst**. Cross the junction with care and turn left, walking down the **High Street**, passing the **New Forest Centre** on your right.

2. At **Beaulieu Road**, turn right and go through the gate next to the cattle grid, then immediately left, signed **Bolton's Bench** – which is the yew tree you can see on top of the hill on your right. Follow the track, passing a car park on your left, then a turning to the cemetery, and continue straight on to a gravel track. Pass

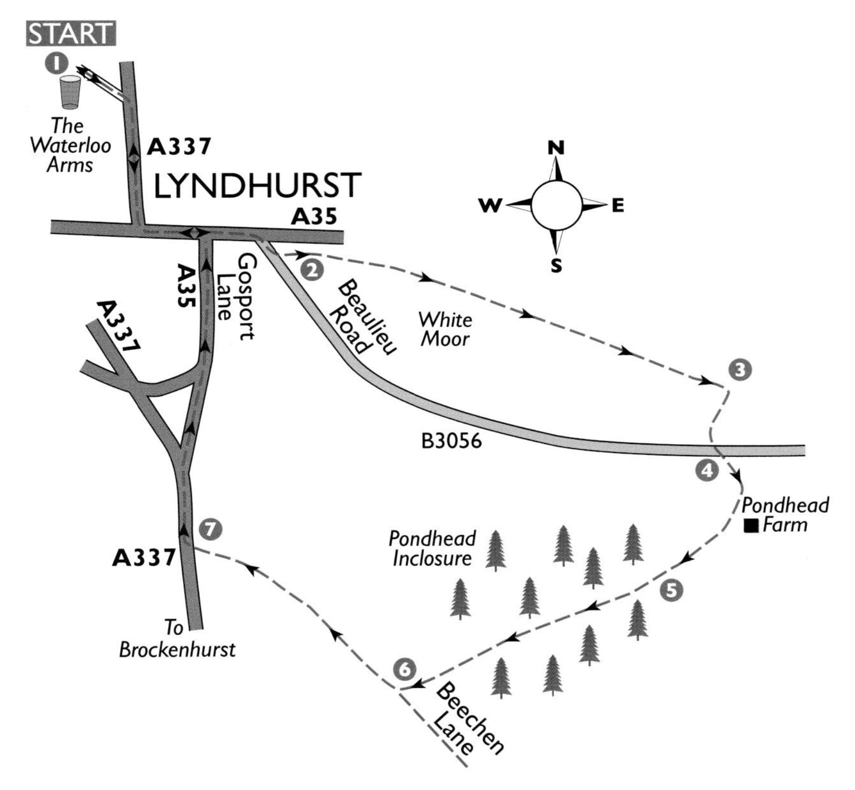

a barrier and continue ahead across the heathland for about a mile.

❸ When you can see Beaulieu Road on your right, look out for a large timber-frame house on the other side of the road and a sign for Lyndhurst. Cross the heath to the road (there are various faint paths you can follow all leading in the same direction).

❹ Cross the road and follow the left-hand surfaced lane, signed **Pondhead Farm**. Stay on this main path, pass a track on your left and cross a bridge over a stream, passing the farm down a track on your left, and keep ahead. Pass a house on your right and walk ahead into the woods.

❺ Now enjoy a shady stretch through woodland glades. Keep going

in the same direction – there are a few paths that you can choose. Soon you will see a very clear gravel cross track ahead of you. This is **Beechen Lane**, an ancient trackway.

6. Turn right and follow Beechen Lane back into Lyndhurst. Go through a gate and walk up to the busy A337, with **Foxlease Girlguiding Activity Centre** in front of you.

7. Turn right and follow the pavement to a junction where you turn right to walk up **Gosport Lane**. This leads to the **High Street**, where you turn left to walk through the village to the junction, then right down **Romsey Road**, and left at **Pikes Hill** to return to the pub and a well earned drink!

Place of Interest Nearby

The **New Forest Centre** in Lyndhurst is a fascinating spot to visit if you want to find out more about the New Forest National Park's history and heritage. In the 13th century, William the Conqueror turned the New Forest into his private hunting ground, preventing the locals from using the forest to graze their livestock, hunt, forage or erect fences. After his death, the 1217 Charter of the Forest, restored the rights of the common people to graze their livestock. Find out more about how the landscape is managed, as well as a programme of events for young families, a free museum, gallery with a year round exhibition programme, gift shop and library. The Centre is next to the main car park.
🌐 newforestcentre.org.uk

Walk 3

BEAULIEU TO BUCKLER'S HARD

Distance: 4½ miles (7.2 km)

Map: OS Explorer OL22 New Forest. **Grid ref:** SU387022

How to get there: South-east from Lyndhurst, follow the B3056 into Beaulieu. Turn left onto Palace Lane and the car park is signed on the right, by the Village Hall. **Sat nav:** SO42 7YA.

Parking: Park in Beaulieu pay and display car park, walk out of the car park and turn right to get to Monty's and the start of the walk.

This route follows the tidal Beaulieu River as it snakes between Beaulieu and the 18th-century village of Buckler's Hard, taking you through shady woods and over boardwalks, with stunning views across the water. Both villages are well worth exploring and are very popular with visitors to the New Forest. Beaulieu dates back to the 13th century, and was built around the abbey, founded in 1204 by Cistercian monks. Buckler's Hard was once a major shipbuilding village, and is now preserved with the opportunity to visit cottages and see exactly what life was like in the time of Nelson.

THE PUB

MONTY'S is the very classy bar of **The Montagu Arms**, in Beaulieu. It serves locally sourced, delicious food and local ale from the Ringwood brewery.
montaguarmshotel.co.uk ☎ 01590 624467.

Alternatively, halfway round the walk is **The Yachtsman's Bar** of **The Master Builder's House Hotel**, by the river at the end of Buckler's Hard village. The view is stunning, with table service from their Breton-clad shipmates. They serve food all day with the menu ranging from salad and light meals to fish and chips.
hillbrookehotels.co.uk/the-master-builders ☎ 01590 616253

The Walk

1. Starting from outside **Monty's**, walk a few metres along **Palace Lane** and next to **The Montagu Arms Hotel** turn right down **Fire Station Lane**, following the sign for the **Solent Way**. Pass the hotel car park and stay on the wide gravel path until you come to a wooden gate. Go through the gate then walk between houses on a gravel track, then by grassland and reed beds, with the woodland giving you occasional shade on a sunny day. Pass **Bailey's Hard** and an information board and continue along the Solent Way.

2. When you come to a sign for the riverside walk, turn left to follow boardwalks by the salt marshes. The river is a designated National

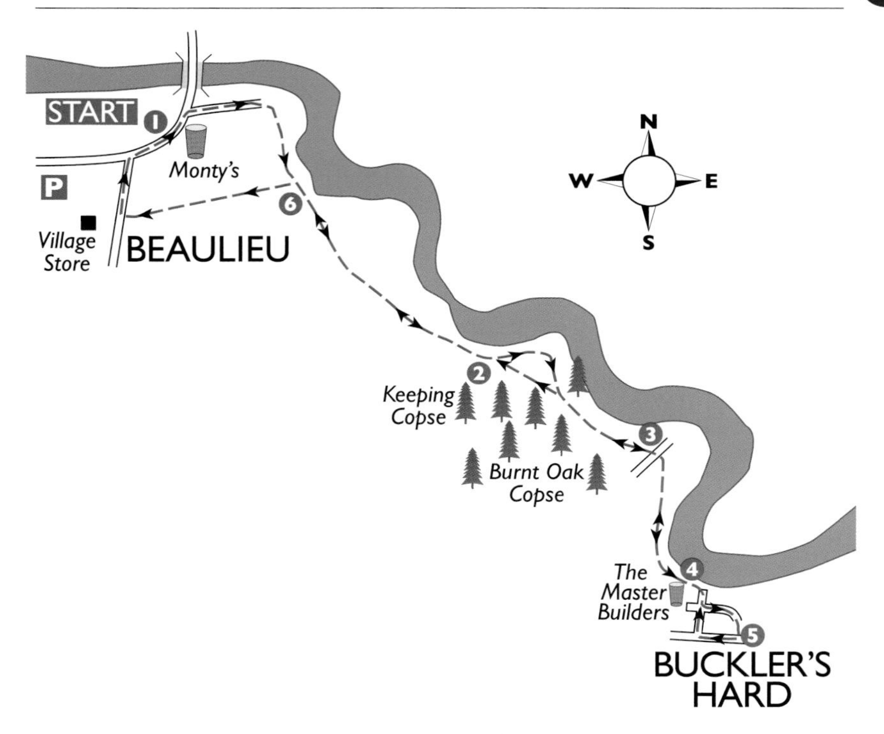

Nature Reserve and this shady stretch gives you fantastic views across the saltings and creeks. You join the main path again and turn left to walk through **Burnt Oak Copse**, where the oak trees date from the early 19th century. Follow the sign to **Buckler's Hard Yacht Harbour** and maritime museum.

3 At a small road, cross over and follow the footpath to **Buckler's Hard**, passing **Beaulieu River Boatyard** and **Duke's Bath House**, a small thatched cottage built by the Duke of Montagu in 1760 for his son who suffered from arthritis.

4 Buckler's Hard has a row of houses on both sides leading down to the river. Turn right and walk up the path, passing the **Yachtsman's Bar** on your right. Then, at the top, turn left and pass the shop and café (this is where you can pay the entrance fee to visit the museum).

5 Walk through the car park and just as you come to the road,

turn right through a kissing gate to walk back through Buckler's Hard. Turn left at the bottom and retrace your steps back along the Solent Way. When you come to the riverside walk option, go straight on to walk by the side of **Keeping Copse**.

6 When you get to the edge of the village, go through a gate to follow the footpath signed to the village. This leads you out onto the **High Street**, with the village shop opposite you. Turn right to return to **Monty's**.

Places of Interest Nearby

Although you can walk through the 18th-century **Buckler's Hard**, where the ships for Nelson's navy were once built, to visit the workers' cottages with their displays depicting life in the 18th century, St Mary's Chapel and the maritime museum, you need to pay the entrance fee. Dogs are welcome on a lead in the grounds only. The village is open daily and it is well worth spending some time there to explore. 🌐 bucklershard.co.uk

The **National Motor Museum** at Beaulieu has everything from F1 cars to Del Boy's Reliant and the 'flying' Ford Anglia from *Harry Potter*. Once you've finished with the cars, there are also the grounds and gardens of Palace House and Beaulieu Abbey to explore. See their website for more details, prices and opening times. 🌐 beaulieu.co.uk

Walk 4

BLASHFORD LAKES AND ROCKFORD COMMON

Distance: 5 miles (8 km)

Map: OS Explorer OL22 New Forest. **Grid ref:** SU159080

How to get there: Follow the A31 to the western edge of the New Forest. Turn right up Gorley Road and the pub is set back from the road on your left. **Sat nav:** BH24 3NA.

Parking: The Alice Lisle pub car park.

Hampshire and Isle of Wight Wildlife Trust manage Blashford Lakes, and these flooded gravel pits make for a good walking contrast to the heathland in the second half of the walk. The lakes are fringed with willow, birch and alder and are an important habitat for overwintering wildfowl, as well as 26 different species of dragonfly. After a relaxing stroll round Blashford Lakes nature reserve, this walk heads off into Rockford Common to explore the New Forest Northern Commons. Rockford Common is managed by the National Trust and is the perfect spot to experience the unique New Forest landscape, one that has been influenced by farmers since the Bronze Age. The mosaic of heather, gorse and woodland has been grazed throughout the centuries by New

Forest ponies, and you are guaranteed to meet plenty of them on this walk. The 5,000 or so ponies in the New Forest help maintain the heathland by preventing saplings from growing and taking over the ground.

THE PUB

THE ALICE LISLE is an impressive country pub in an idyllic rural setting, owned by Fuller's. It has a large car park, beer garden and conservatory, so you should be able to find a spot, even on a busy summer's weekend. Make sure you get your table number though before ordering food. Inside, the pub is tastefully decorated with large slate tiles and oriental rugs. It is hard to imagine it being anything other than a pub, but up to the 1960s this was actually the village school. Look out for a series of framed newspaper stories inside, telling the tragic tale of Alice Lisle, the last woman in England to be beheaded, in 1685. The food is delicious.

🌐 thealicelisle.co.uk ☎ 01425 474700

The Walk

1 From the pub car park, walk down to the road and turn right. Follow the side of the green in front of the pub, cross a cattle grid, and at the end of a brick garden wall, just past **Ivy Cottage**, turn right through a gate.

2 A narrow path leads you for about 100 metres to the side of **Blashford Lake**, which you can glimpse through the hedge on your left. Stay on the path as it veers left, and as you walk look out for sailing boats on the lake. When you reach the gate for **Spinnaker Sailing Club**, follow the path to the right, then, turn left just after the club entrance, through a metal gate, with a sign for the **Avon Valley Path**. Follow the path with the lake on your left. Eventually you walk by the side of houses, then a kissing gate.

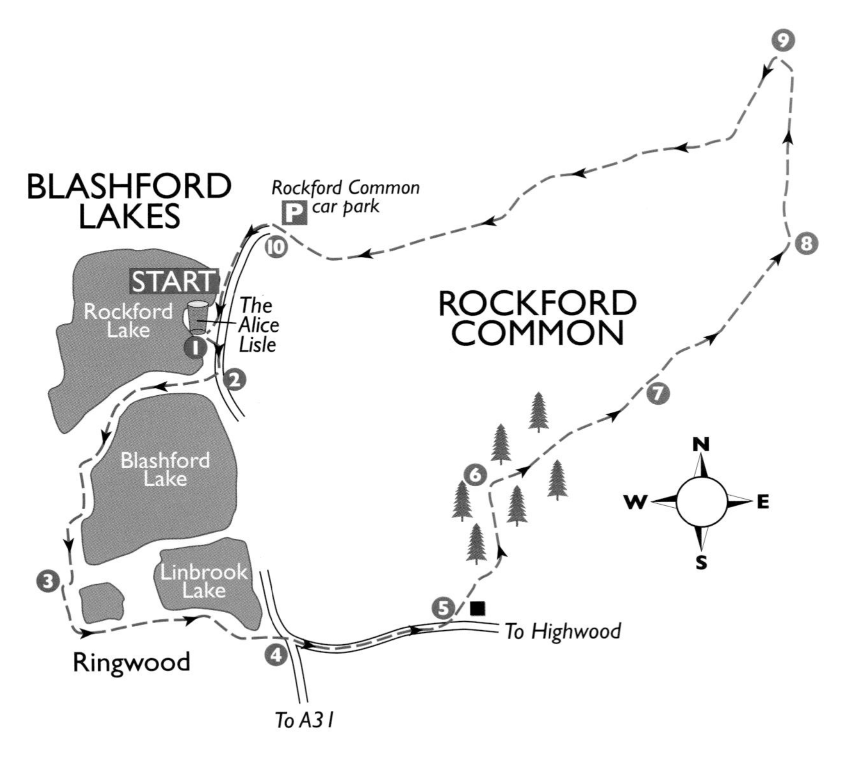

3 Go through the gate and turn right, then after a short stretch left, go through another kissing gate, still on the Avon Valley Path. Stay on this path until you come to a telegraph pole. Now leave the Avon Valley Path and turn left. Stay on this shady path, passing a small footbridge on your right, until you come to a road.

4 Turn right at the road. Bear left at the T-junction, following the sign for **Highwood**. Follow the road with a stream on your right.

5 When you come to a large thatched cottage set back from the road on your left, with a log with the name '**Exley**' on it, turn left to follow the signed footpath next to the house and up into the trees. There is a useful boardwalk at the start of the path that keeps you out of the mud. As the path begins to lead uphill, you come to a farm gate across the path with a footpath sign. Go through the gate then turn left for a short, steeper section. Go straight ahead at a crossroads of tracks, passing a sign on the tree for '**Tanglewood**'.

6 At the next crossroads of tracks, turn right, just past a house called **Foxglove Corner**. Head downhill, passing **Yew Tree Cottage** on one side of the track, and Lavender Farm on the other. At the bottom of the hill, cross a track and continue straight on, passing farm buildings on your left.

7 Pass **Furzie Field** on the right and continue in the same direction through the trees. The path can get muddy here, so if it's easier walk either side of the path. Continue until you pass under telegraph wires and find yourself in heathland. Walk straight ahead, passing **Waterslade Farm** over to your right. You are heading for a long gravel track that you will shortly see ahead of you.

8 When you get to the track, turn left and follow it until it turns to the left. At this point, leave the track and walk past the barrier. Continue in the same direction, straight over at the cross tracks then when the path is about to go steeply downhill, turn left and walk past a small pit on your right.

9 Turn left at the edge of the pit, then follow this undulating path until you come to a cross track where you turn right. When the path splits, take the higher option. Follow the high path, making the most of the views across the heath. When you come to a wide; surfaced track, head downhill under the trees and through the barrier to walk through the car park.

10 Walk down to the stream and turn left, following the road sign to **Rockford**. Follow the Avon Valley Path as you walk along the verge on the right-hand side of the road. At a T-junction, cross the road and go through a gate to a narrow path. Walk ahead and through the gate to **The Alice Lisle**.

Place of Interest Nearby

The **Ringwood Brewery** tour experience takes about 1½ hours, with no children allowed under the age of 8. It includes a complimentary drink, tour of the brewery where you can taste the malted barleys and sniff the hops, and a visit to the Tun Room to see the fermentations bubbling away. 🌐 ringwoodbrewery.co.uk

Walk 5

HALE AND NEW FOREST VILLAGES

Distance: 5¾ miles (9.2 km)

Map: OS Explorer OL22 New Forest. **Grid ref:** SU187175

How to get there: On the north-western edge of the New Forest, 10 miles south of Salisbury. Follow the A338 to The Borough, then the B3080 and the car park is signed on your left. **Sat nav:** SP6 2QZ.

Parking: Free parking in the National Trust Hale Purlieu car park.

This peaceful walk explores delightful villages and woodland on the northern border of the New Forest, in the valley of the River Avon. A section of the walk follows the long-distance walking trail the Avon Valley Path, a 34-mile linear route taking you from Salisbury Cathedral, 10 miles north of here, to Christchurch Priory and the sea. Highlights of the walk include the grounds of the Palladian-style Georgian mansion, Hale House, thatched cottages on the village green, and the woods of Stricklands

Plantation. There are also plenty of New Forest ponies to spot, grazing hedgerows, or nonchalantly standing in the middle of a narrow road, testing the patience of waiting car drivers.

THE PUB **THE HORSE AND GROOM** in Woodgreen is conveniently in the middle of this walk, and a lovely spot to pass some time sitting at the tables in front, watching the ponies wander down the High Street. This family-run pub serves good food and is dog and family friendly. No website ☎ 01725 510739

The Walk

1. From the car park, walk up to the road and turn right. Walk with a view across **Hale Purlieu** on your right and just after the power-lines turn left through a large metal gate to follow the byway (for over a decade the National Grid have been planning to move the pylons underground – so if you don't spot them, they've finally done it!).

2. Turn right and follow the track past rhododendron bushes to a fingerpost and cross-junction at the bottom of the hill. Now turn direct right along the narrow bridleway, heading gently downhill for about ½ mile until you come to a gate. Go through the gate and turn left along the lane. Just before the house **'Merry Mole'** and a right-hand bend, turn left up a track with small wooden posts either side of you. The path veers to the left again and shortly takes you into the village of **Hatchet Green**.

3. Cross the car park in front of the village hall and then turn left along a surfaced track across the delightful village green, passing the **Millennium Stone** on your left and heading for a thatched cottage. At the cottage (**Old Dame's School**) turn right and walk up to the road junction.

4. Turn left and walk by the side of this quiet road, crossing a cattle grid, then continue for about ¾ mile, following the **Avon Valley Path**, with sweeping views across the valley on your right. Pass **Home Farm Cottage**, then **Home Farm**. The road turns left then you come to a sign for **St Mary's Church**, next to the sweeping drive up to **Hale House**.

❺ Go through the gate and follow the path with the lime-tree-lined drive on your left. As you get close to the house, with a fairy-tale-style well in front of you, follow the track to the right, then left, always staying on the Avon Valley Path, and passing St Mary's Church to reach **Moot Lane**.

❻ *It is well worth crossing the lane to the bridge and admiring the view on either side of the River Avon.* At Moot Lane turn left, then turn right at the junction signed **Woodgreen** and **Breamore**. Pass

Rivermead, and go left up the surfaced drive, still following the Avon Valley Path. Cross the stile just to the right of the entrance to **North End**. Now walk across the edge of three fields.

7 When you cross the stile out of the last field, keep ahead along the track. It bears left, then right at the junction to a road at **Woodgreen Common**. This is a beautiful spot and very popular with the local ponies. Turn right down the road. Pass a lane on the left and 30mph signs on the road. Now follow a permissive path on the right of the road. Turn right through a gate and follow the permissive path to reach the village shop and tearoom. This shop is perfect for stocking up on delicious local cakes! Turn left at the road, passing the village hall, and ahead at the junction to the **Horse and Groom** pub on the left.

8 Just after the pub, follow the road to the left. At the T-junction turn left over a stile by a cattle grid and drive to a thatched cottage. Follow the enclosed path, then continue up the gravel drive to cross a stile by a gate. Turn left along the lane for 25 metres and then right, following a gravel track with houses on the right. Where the track swings right, continue straight on across the common, passing between the cricket pitch and the thatched clubhouse.

9 Go through a gate in the fence on the right. Follow the path down through the woods of **Godshill Inclosure**, cross the stream to a junction, then keep ahead uphill until you come to a cross track surrounded by tall pines.

10 Turn left and then shortly turn left again to follow the cycle track for a level stretch of walking through the trees. Go through a gate, cross the lane and follow the track opposite. At the gated entrance to **North Densome House**, turn right and follow the footpath as

it skirts the grounds of the house. Cross two small footbridges, then a stile and cross the field to a stile on the other side.

⓫ At the track turn right, then at the road turn left to return to the car park.

Place of Interest Nearby

Hale Purlieu is a stunning area of lowland heath, managed by the National Trust. There are wonderful views from the car park across the landscape. If you want to explore its valleys, woodland and mires, the National Trust have a 3-mile figure-of-eight walk, starting from the car park, that would take you just over an hour to do. 🌐 nationaltrust.org.uk and search 'Hale Purlieu' for the directions.

Walk 6
MOTTISFONT

Distance: 3 miles (4.8 km)

Map: OS Explorer 131 Romsey, Andover & Test Valley.
Grid ref: SU318261

How to get there: Dunbridge is 5 miles north of Romsey, with the pub by the train station in the centre of the village.
Sat nav: SO51 0LF.

Parking: The Mill Arms car park.

This walk explores ancient woodland and fields, before heading south to cross the water meadows of Dunbridge Springs, by the River Dun. Boardwalks save your boots from getting muddy after rain. A visit afterwards to the stunning Mottisfont Abbey is the perfect finish to a peaceful day in the English countryside. The woodland dates back over 400 years and is an important habitat for flora and fauna. There are sheep and cows in some of the fields, but plenty of space crossing the water meadows for a dog to stretch its legs.

THE PUB

THE MILL ARMS is beautifully decorated inside, with leather sofas and open fires. This 18th-century former coaching inn also has a lovely garden area for sunny days. They serve a wide range of real ales and have separate lunch and dinner menus, ranging from light bites to Sunday roasts. It is also the recipient of a TripAdvisor Certificate of Excellence.

🌐 millarmsdunbridge.co.uk ☎ 01794 340355

The Walk

1 Cross the road in front of the pub and walk over the train tracks, passing the station for **Mottisfont and Dunbridge** and following the road sign to **Mottisfont**. Just after the 40 mph sign, turn right through a gate into the field, signed to **Mottisfont Abbey**.

2 Walk diagonally left up the field, heading for a large oak tree and a kissing gate halfway along the edge of the field. Go through the gate then diagonally across the next field, then go through another gate and head down to **Hatt Lane**. Cross the lane and go through the gate opposite, and walk diagonally across the next field, following the field path.

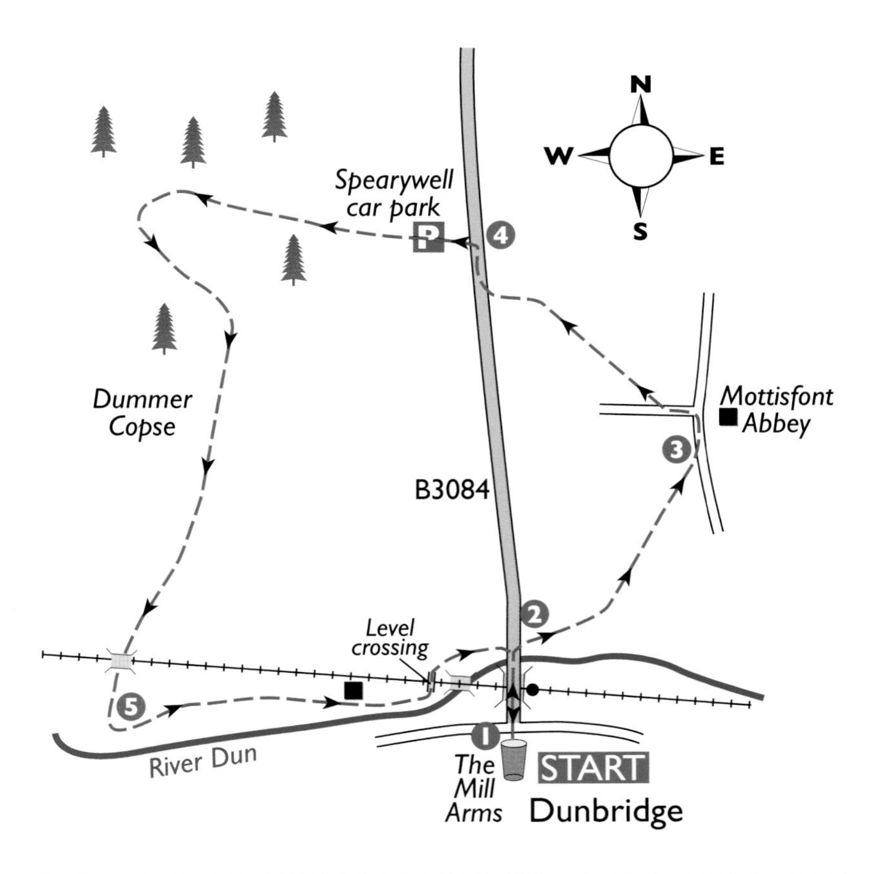

3 At the end of the field, walk down to the road and turn left, passing **Abbey Farm cottages**. Opposite the gates to **Mottisfont Abbey**, turn left down **Bengers Lane** and almost immediately, just before the national speed limit signs, turn right to follow the footpath diagonally across the fields until you come to the B3084.

4 Cross the road then turn right and walk with care by the side of the road, heading north for a short distance to the **National Trust Spearywell car park** on your left. Walk through the car park to follow the gravel path through the woods. Pass a sign for Spearywell car park and take a left turn at a T-junction,

following the path out of the woods. Look out for a stone marker at a junction to keep you on the right track. At the edge of the wood turn right on a hedged path between fields. Cross a short boardwalk and go under a railway bridge.

5 Stay on the path until you get to the banks of the **River Dun**, where you turn left through a kissing gate to cross the water meadows of **Dunbridge Springs**, with the river on your right and boardwalks over the wetter spots. Cross a stile and follow the path past a small thatched cottage, then through a kissing gate. Follow the side of the field and a track, keeping left at a large oak tree and broken stile. Pass an electricity substation then cross the railway with care and follow the track until you find yourself back at the road on the northern edge of **Dunbridge**. Turn right and cross the railway to return to the pub.

Place of Interest Nearby

Mottisfont Abbey is an 18th-century house with a medieval priory by the banks of the River Test. It is best known for its stunning walled rose garden, which is a feast to the senses in June. Dogs on a lead are allowed in the gardens.
🌐 nationaltrust.org.uk/mottisfont

Walk 7

TITCHFIELD CANAL & THE SOLENT WAY

Distance: 6 miles (9.6 km)

Map: OS Explorer 119 Meon Valley. **Grid ref:** SU541055

How to get there: Titchfield is just west of Fareham, off junction 9 of the M27. Follow the A27 into the village, then head south and turn left at Coach Hill to Bridge Street. Cross the bridge over the canal and the car park is immediately on your right. **Sat nav:** PO14 4EA.

Parking: Bridge Street Car Park.

Titchfield is a delightful spot to explore, with timber-framed houses, quaint cottages and St Peter's Church reputed to be the oldest church in Hampshire, while the village itself dates back to the 6th century. The footpath by the canal follows the edge of Titchfield Haven National Nature Reserve, before heading west by the coast along the Solent Way. The return crosses fields back to the village. There are a couple of stiles along the route.

THE PUB

THE QUEENS HEAD is a friendly, traditional pub with exposed brick walls, wooden beams and an open fire, plus a small beer garden behind for sunny days. The menu includes locally sourced food, with sausages and pies from Hadlows of Titchfield, and New Forest ice cream. The beers are also locally sourced, with a rotating choice of four real ales.

🌐 queenshead-titchfield.co.uk ☎ 01329 842154

The Walk

1. From the car park, turn left and walk by the canal, through a kissing gate and follow the footpath (point 3). But if you want to visit the pub first, come out of the car park up to **Bridge Street**, then left. At the mini roundabout turn right into **South Street**, passing timber-framed cottages. Continue straight on to **High Street**, where the road widens and the pub is at the top on the left.

2. Turn right out of the pub and walk back down the **High Street**, then left down narrow **Church Street**. Take the path to the right of the church which leads you over the canal. Then turn right to follow the canal path, signed **'Lower Meon Valley Trail'**.

3. After a detour to the pub or walking straight from the car park, you will now find yourself heading south along the **Titchfield Canal** for 2 miles, following the edge of **Titchfield Haven**, past fields, then woods and finally marshes as you get closer to the sea. Cross a meadow to a kissing gate, following the signposted right of way and passing a sign for Titchfield Haven. Then go right through the gate to **Meon Road**.

4. Cross the road and go through the gate opposite, passing **Meon Shore Chalets** to follow the **Solent Way**. The path starts to head slightly uphill, passing **Cliff Cottages**. Walk along the cliff tops

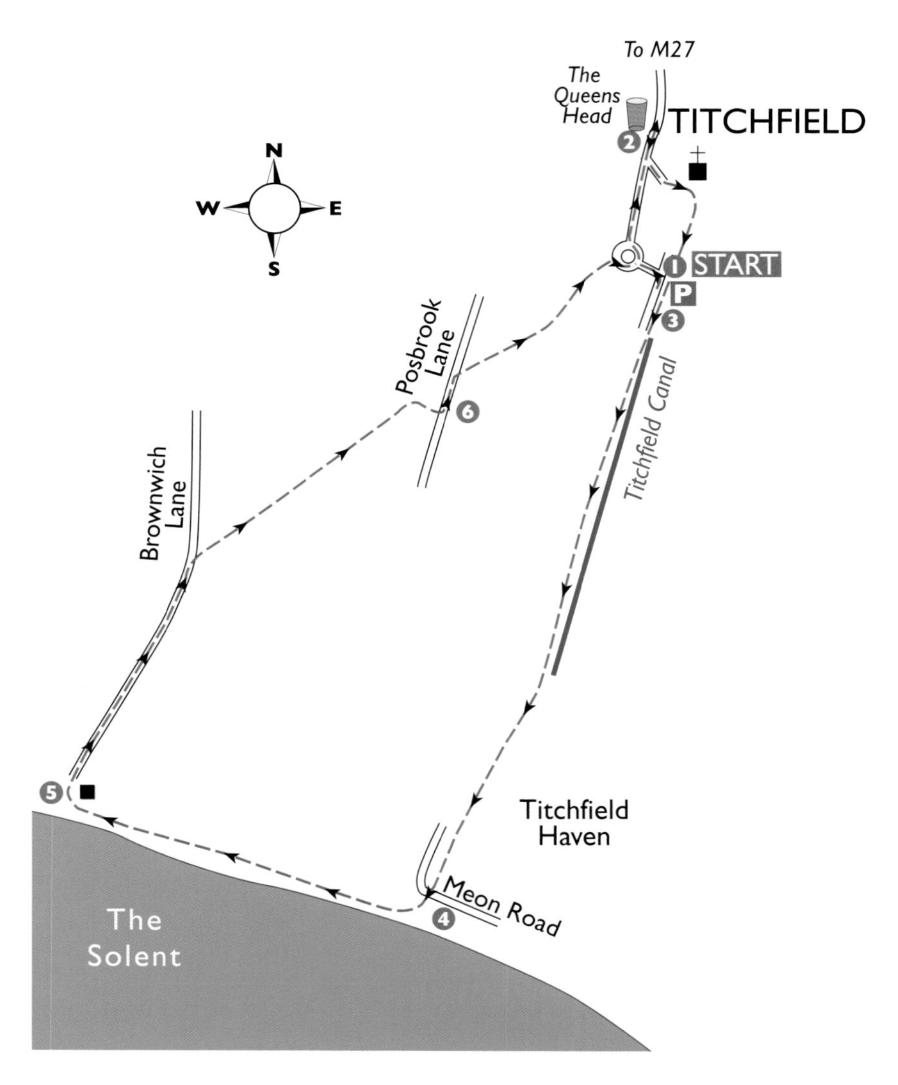

for about ½ mile, enjoying the view, until you head downhill, passing **Sea House** on your right to **Brownwich Lane**.

5 Turn right and follow the surfaced lane. After about ¾ mile, by red brick farm buildings, turn right and follow the footpath round the field, heading back towards **Titchfield**. When you come to a large house on your left, turn right and follow **Heath Lane**. Go through a kissing gate to **Posbrook Lane**.

6 Turn left and walk by the side of this quiet lane, passing **Barn Close**. By a lamp post on your right, go over the stile and follow the footpath diagonally right across the field and through a metal kissing gate. You are now at the edge of Titchfield, pass garages and along a narrow alley between the houses, then walk up **Lower Bellfield**. At the top, turn right onto **Coach Hill**, then at the mini roundabout, turn right again onto **Bridge Street** to return to your car (or left into the village for the pub).

Place of Interest Nearby

Half a mile north of the village along the A27, are the ruins of the 13th-century **Titchfield Abbey**, in the valley of the River Meon. Following the Dissolution of the Monasteries in the 16th century, Henry VIII gave the Abbey to the Earl of Southampton, who transformed the building into a grand Tudor mansion. He had a large gatehouse built across the nave of the former monastic church, which is still standing today. The site is managed by English Heritage, is free to visit and open daily.
🌐 english-heritage.org.uk

Walk 8

Old Winchester Hill

Distance: 8 miles (12.8 km)

Map: OS Explorer OL32 Winchester. **Grid ref:** SU624231

How to get there: Warnford is 10 miles south-east of Winchester. Follow the A272, then take a right turn to Lane End from where a narrow road leads to the village. **Sat nav:** SO32 3LB.

Parking: There is a large car park behind the pub.

This is an exhilarating walk in the footsteps of history as it follows the trackbed of the old 'Strawberry Line', that from 1903 to 1968 ran between Portsmouth and London, transporting train loads of fruit when Hampshire was the centre for market gardening. The South Downs Way heads up to explore the Iron Age hillfort on top of Old Winchester Hill, with panoramic views across this ancient landscape. It is also an excellent spot for birdwatching as

red kite and buzzards hover over the scrub and chalk grassland. Your return is along the Monarch's Way, following the escape route of King Charles II after his defeat in 1651 at the Battle of Worcester. There are some steep up and downhill sections at Old Winchester Hill, but the views will make it all worthwhile. Dogs need to be on a lead on the hill as it is grazed by sheep.

THE PUB

THE GEORGE AND FALCON is a large, wood-panelled pub with seating options to suit all tastes - in the bar, snug or dining areas, with a log fire for winter walkers and a delightful riverside garden bordered by the River Meon for warmer days. They offer a carvery on Sundays and the service is fast and friendly. The building dates back to the 16th century with dogs and walkers welcome.

georgeandfalcon.com ☎ 01730 829623

The Walk

1 With your back to the **George and Falcon** pub, turn left, cross the A32 with care then head up **Hayden Lane**, following the brown sign for **Old Winchester Hill**. This narrow road leads you uphill, initially past cottages, until you leave the village behind

you and the gradient levels off. When you come to a bridge over the old trackbed, turn left and follow the footpath sign for about 20 metres, then take the path on the right that leads down the steep bank to reach the old **Meon Valley railway track**.

2 Turn right and walk back under the bridge to follow the straight path ahead. The shady banks are carpeted with hart's tongue fern, which soon gives way to trees as the trackbed leads up to give a wonderful view either side across the Meon valley. Cross **Peake New Road** and continue along the track until you come to a fingerpost for the **South Downs Way** on your right.

3 Turn left and follow the path as it zigzags down the bank with a wooden fence on your left. Pass a metal farm gate then turn right to follow the fenced path of the South Downs Way, leading away from the track towards Old Winchester Hill, with open fields on your left. The path shortly turns sharp left and begins to head uphill. Ignore a fingerpost for the **Monarch's Way**, and go through a gate then up to the top of the hill.

4 From the top of Old Winchester Hill you can immediately see why this spot was chosen by Iron Age man to be a hillfort, as you can see for miles across the surrounding countryside. Walk ahead, past the viewpoint, pass a bench on your left and walk through a metal swing gate, with a footpath sign for the **South Downs Way** on your right. Follow the path ahead, admiring the view, until you come to a gate on your right for a car park and a small information hut in front with story boards explaining the site's history.

5 Just before the hut there is an information board, where you turn left and follow the narrow grass path, then turn right and go through a metal swing gate. Now follow the green circular walk arrow as it leads you steeply downhill to a narrow cross path where you turn left. Go through a metal gate as the path leads you through a shady patch of woods and up wooden steps, then through another gate before a short but very steep stretch back up the hill. You will be rewarded at the top by spectacular views!

6 Don't go through the gate at the top of the hill, instead turn right, following the sign for the hillfort and along a narrow path

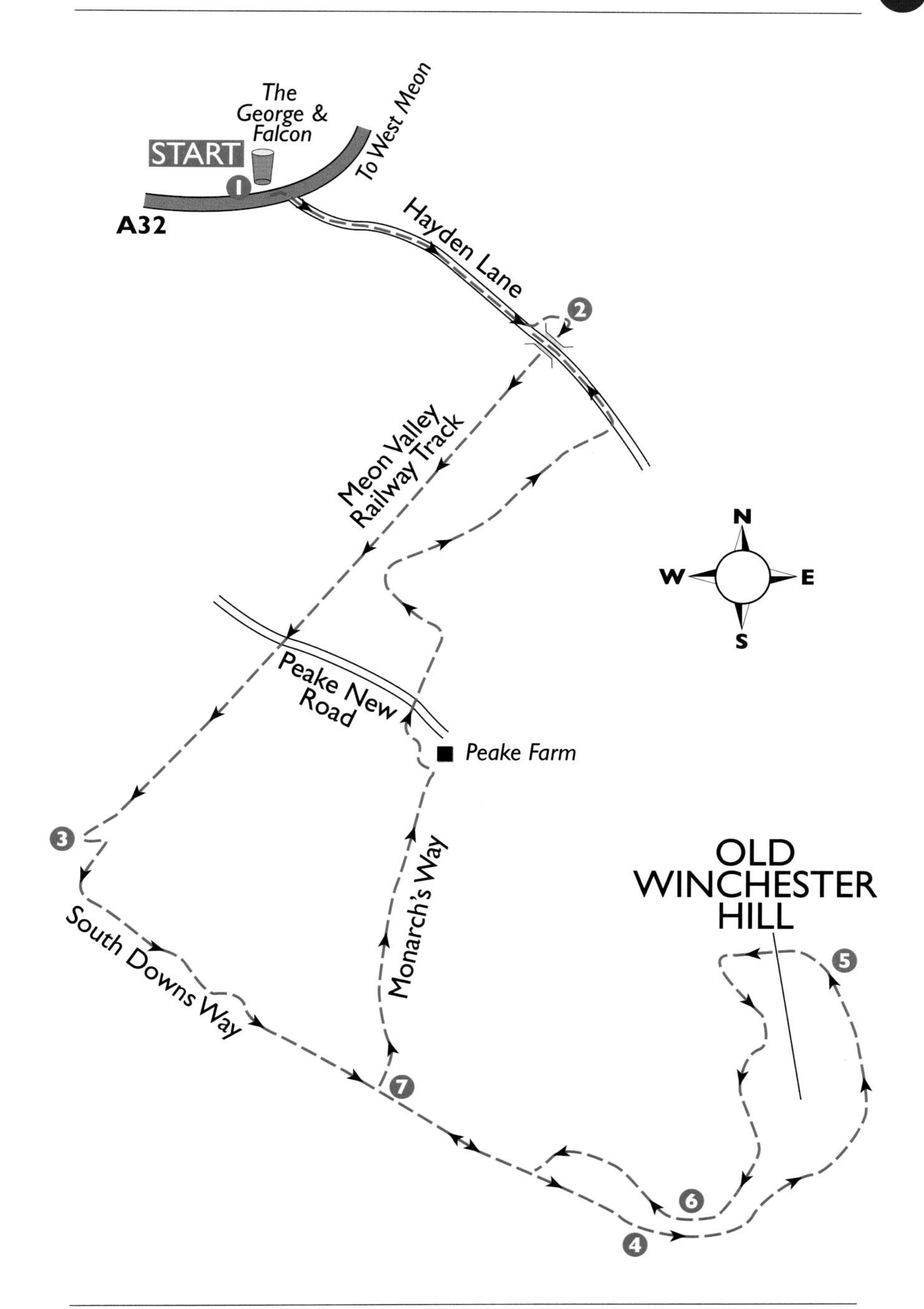
The
George &
Falcon
START
To West Meon
A32
Hayden Lane
Meon Valley
Railway Track
N
W
E
S
Peake New
Road
Peake Farm
Monarch's Way
South Downs Way
OLD
WINCHESTER
HILL

that snakes around the hill with a steep drop to your right. Go up more wooden steps to a gate and you will find yourself back on top of the hill. Now turn right and follow the lower path round the embankments, rather than heading left towards the viewpoint you were at earlier. Turn right and retrace your steps, through the gate and downhill to the fingerpost.

7 Turn right to follow the **Monarch's Way**. The path leads you across fields and round **Peake Farm**, over **Peake New Road**, then past paddocks running parallel with the **Meon Valley Railway path** over on your left. Eventually you come to **Hayden Lane**. Turn left and walk back to Warnford, passing the bridge over the old railway bed and heading downhill to cross the A32 to the pub.

Place of Interest Nearby

This walk takes you to the top of **Old Winchester Hill**. You can shorten the route by a few miles by walking up to the top, admiring the view across the valley to Beacon Hill, then walking back down again. But it is well worth exploring for as well as the stunning views, this site is rich in archaeology from the Mesolithic Age when Stone Age hunter-gathers roamed the hill, right up to the Second World War. The Iron Age hillfort has left the most distinct mark, but there are also earlier Bronze Age barrows or burial mounds. Smaller hollows date back to the Second World War, when the army used the hill as a mortar firing range.

Walk 9
HINTON AMPNER

Distance: 4 miles (6.4 km)

Map: OS Explorer OL32 Winchester. **Grid ref:** SU590278

How to get there: Hinton Ampner is 8 miles east of Winchester, leave the M3 at exit 9 and follow the signs to Petersfield. **Sat nav:** SO24 0NH.

Parking: There is a large car park at The Hinton Arms.

Walking with views across the estate of the National Trust's Hinton Ampner, this route follows part of the Wayfarer's Walk, passing an unspoilt landscape with grazing sheep and majestic beech trees. There are stiles in the middle of the walk and I would recommend leaving your dog at home this time. This would also give you the chance to explore Hinton Ampner, for as well as walking through the estate, the end of the walk takes you right past the entrance to this elegant country house. There are also some lovely estate cottages to admire in the village, as you head back to The Hinton Arms at the end of the walk.

THE PUB

THE HINTON ARMS is a privately owned traditional pub, with an excellent children's play area at the back of the large beer garden and horses in the field beyond. It serves locally-sourced food seven days a week and is renowned for its large portions. Dogs are only allowed in the bar area.
hintonarms.co.uk ☎01962 771252

Two minutes away by car is **The Flower Pots** in Cheriton, which has won Southern Hampshire Camra's *Pub of the Year* so is worth a visit for beer drinkers. It also serves delicious food.
flowerpotscheriton.co.uk ☎ 01962 771318

The Walk

1. From the **Hinton Arms** pub, turn left and walk along **Petersfield Road**, then turn left down **Kilmeston Road**. When you get to a patch of trees on your left, just as the road bends to the right, turn left to follow the **Restricted Byway** to a swing gate.

2. Turn right through the gate and follow the footpath arrows across the fields, heading south-west along the **Wayfarer's Walk**. Cross a stile to a narrow road.

3. Turn right for a few metres, then turn left to continue along the Wayfarer's Walk, opposite the gates to **Kilmeston Manor**. Cross three stiles and continue along the path, passing under some magnificent beech trees.

4. When you come to a road, turn left. Pass a small triangular green on your right and **Pond Cottage** on your left. Turn right just past the cottage to follow the footpath sign, then left through a patch of trees. Ignore a cross path and continue in the same direction between the fields. At the field edge turn left, still following the footpath and stay on the path as you cross the fields. The path leads you down to a narrow hedged path, where you turn left and walk to the road.

5. Turn left and follow the road until you find yourself back at the

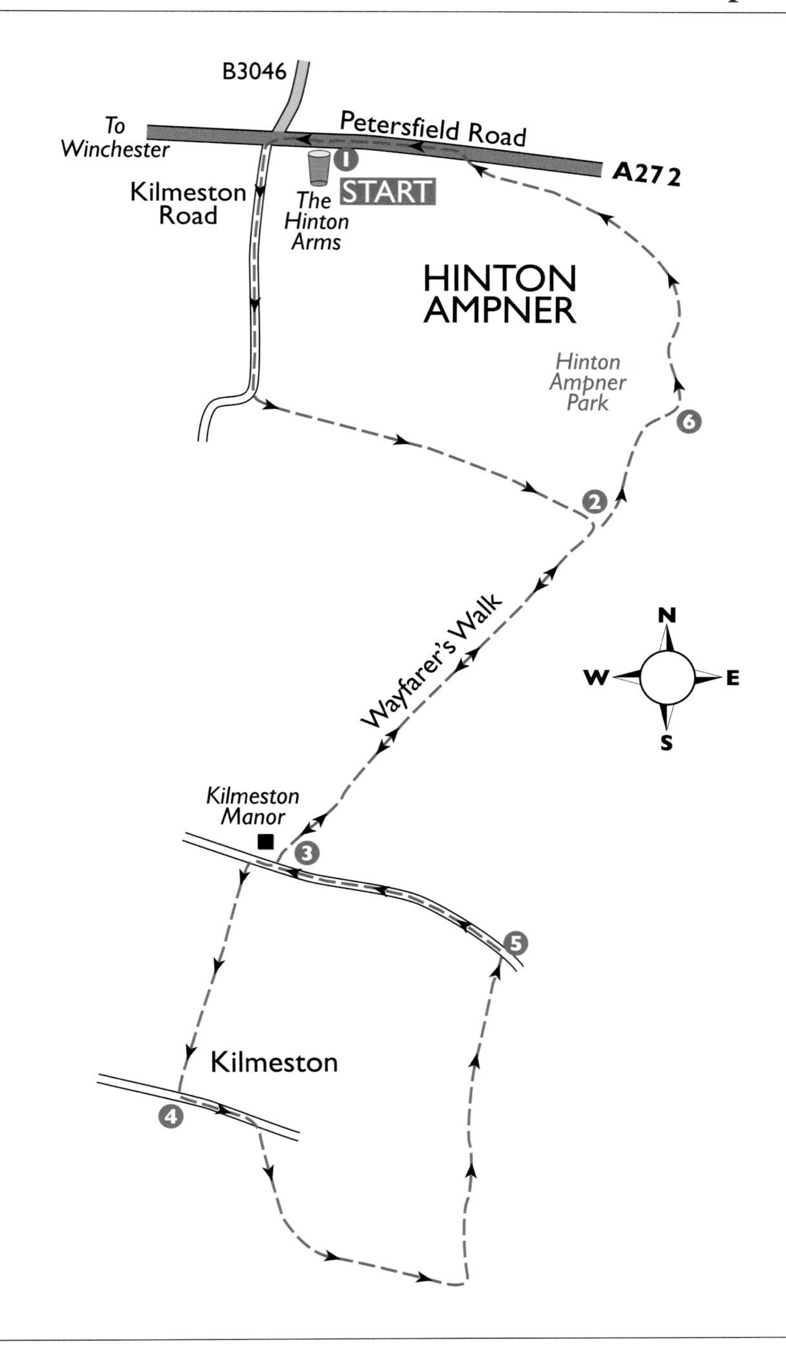
B3046
To Winchester
Petersfield Road
A272
1
START
The Hinton Arms
Kilmeston Road
HINTON AMPNER
Hinton Ampner Park
6
2
Wayfarer's Walk
N
W
E
S
Kilmeston Manor
3
5
Kilmeston
4

stile at point 3. Cross back over the stile and retrace your steps along the Wayfarer's Walk until you come to the swing gate. But don't turn left, instead go straight on up a short path and through a gate with arrows for the footpath.

6 Follow a fenced path straight on, then head left through a gate to find yourself in front of the church, with **Hinton Ampner house** on your left. Turn right to once more follow the Wayfarer's Walk. Just past the cottages, turn left over a stile, following the footpath sign. Head diagonally down across **Hinton Ampner Park**, heading left towards the road. Cross a cattle grid at the drive to **Hinton Ampner**, then turn left and follow the road back to the pub.

Place of Interest Nearby

There has been a manor house at **Hinton Ampner** since Tudor times. The original house was demolished in 1793, although some traces still remain, including the stables that now house a National Trust café. A Georgian house replaced the Tudor manor, which in turn was encased in an elaborate Tudor Gothic extension in the 1860s, although with no bathrooms, as the owner had once caught a cold from recklessly using a bathroom and had hated them ever since. The house you now see is Neo-Georgian and was converted from the former building in the 1930s, with bathrooms added. 🌐 nationaltrust.org.uk/hintonampner

Walk 10

WINCHESTER'S WATER MEADOWS

Distance: 5 miles (8 km)

Map: OS Explorer OL32 Winchester. **Grid ref:** SU475272

How to get there: The A34 starts in Winchester and the M3 runs along its eastern edge. From exit 11 of the M3, take the A3090 to St Cross Road, with Five Bridges Road on the right. **Sat nav:** SO23 9RU.

Parking: Roadside along Five Bridges Road. If there are no spaces, city centre car parks The Brooks (SO23 8QY) and Friarsgate (SO23 8BQ) are both a 5 minute walk from point 6 of the walk.

The picturesque water meadows to the east of Winchester were created in the 18th century, when the Itchen Navigation was busy with barges transporting coal and timber from Southampton to Winchester, to fuel the industrial revolution. Now they are a popular spot with picnicking families and grazed by docile cows. They also offer fine views of the Hospital of St Cross, founded by Henry of Blois, grandson of William the Conqueror. The Almshouses were added to the existing hospital buildings in the 15th century. The middle of the walk explores the historic heart of Winchester, first passing Wolvesey Castle, the medieval palace of the powerful bishops of Winchester, Winchester College founded in 1382, and one of the largest cathedrals in Europe. The beloved Regency author, Jane Austen, spent the last few weeks of her life in Winchester. Her funeral was held in the Cathedral itself in 1817, and she was buried in its north aisle. King Alfred was the founding father of Winchester and his imposing bronze statue, designed by Hamo Thornycroft, was erected in 1899. The romantic poet John Keats spent a few weeks in Winchester, with its water meadows an inspiration for *To Autumn*. At any time of year, this level walk is a wonderful option for an easy waterside stroll and a unique pub.

THE PUB

THE WYKEHAM ARMS lies between the Cathedral and the 14th-century college, and is full of character. Enter its bow doors to find a quirky pub packed with artefacts, ranging from old school desks with ink wells in the bar to Thomas Crapper vintage loos in the bathroom. It serves a seasonal mix of locally sourced food and is also dog friendly. The former landlord was a collector and his eclectic mix of various objects still adorn the walls. Definitely worth a visit.

🌐 wykehamarmswinchester.co.uk ☎ 01962 853834

The Walk

1. Head down **Five Bridges Road** away from the main road, to turn left on a wide path signed '**The Hospital of St Cross**'. After about 100 metres, this leads to a gate and footpath, again signed for the hospital. Walk with the **River Itchen** on your right, until you reach the brick walls behind the Hospital of St Cross.

2. Keep ahead to a swing gate into a field, with the river on your right at the edge of a meadow. Ignore a path to the left and continue ahead and over a small footbridge into **St Faith Meadow**, with a good view of **St Catherine's Hill** up on your right.

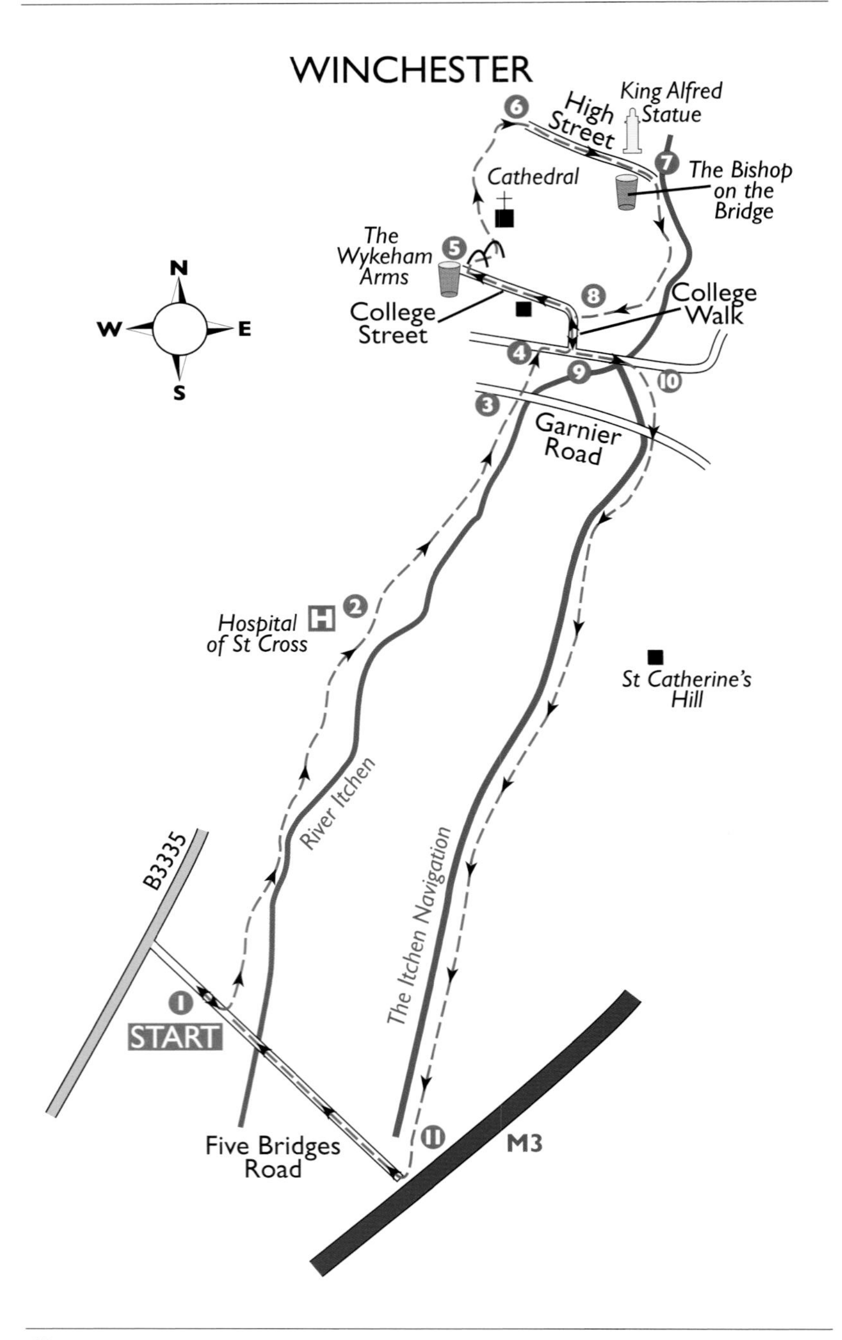
WINCHESTER
King Alfred Statue
High Street
The Bishop on the Bridge
Cathedral
The Wykeham Arms
College Street
College Walk
N
W
E
S
Garnier Road
Hospital of St Cross
St Catherine's Hill
River Itchen
The Itchen Navigation
B3335
START
Five Bridges Road
M3

3 When you reach **Garnier Road**, cross and continue along the footpath by the bridge, signed '**City Centre**', '**Cathedral**' and '**Tourist Information**'.

4 At the next road, follow the road right, then go left following **College Walk** and the sign for **Wolvesey Castle**. Turn left again onto **College Street**, passing the castle ruins on your right. Look out for the blue plaque above the door of 8 College Street, where Jane Austen spent the last few weeks of her life.

5 At the end of the road, look out for the wonderful **Wykeham Arms**, tucked away on your left. Turn right, walking under the arches and ancient city gates, passing the **Church of St Swithun upon Kingsgate**. Turn right and walk under another arch to the Cathedral, passing timber-framed **Cheyne Court** in **Cathedral Close**. Head for a passage to the left of the Cathedral which leads you to the large Cathedral green and war memorial.

6 There are two paths leading into the city centre – take the path with the Cathedral on your right and the war memorial on your left, passing the **William Walker pub** to the pedestrianised **High Street**. There are often market stalls down the centre of this road. Turn right and head for the **statue of King Alfred**, which you can spot ahead of you in the distance.

7 Walk past the statue and pass the **Bishop on the Bridge Pub** (note **Winchester City Mill** on your left), then turn right to follow the **River Itchen**, passing **St Mary Magdalen Almshouses**.

8 The river disappears under the large brick '**Benday Developments**', with a plaque telling you that there has been a mill at this point since the 12th century. Turn right for a few metres, then left to follow the sign to the water meadows. Pass **Wolvesey Castle** again then turn left and retrace your steps down College Walk. Turn left and cross the bridge.

9 At the end of this road, turn right to follow the '**Itchen Navigation**' footpath sign along **Viaduct Way**. Just past **1 New Bridge Cottage**, take the path down some steps to the side of the river.

⑩ Follow the river past houses then fields, following the **Pilgrims' Trail** for 1 mile. Cross the road and continue straight on, passing a small car park on your left. Then follow the surfaced path with the river down on your right. You eventually pass the gate to **St Catherine's Hill Nature Reserve**, where if you have the energy you could head up the steps to admire the view.

⑪ Otherwise continue ahead until you come to an attractively carved curved bench. Walk under the railway bridge. Then look out for a sign on your right, signed for '**St Cross**' and '**Stanmore**'. Take this path to return to **Five Bridges Road**.

Place of Interest Nearby

The historic **Winchester City Mill** is a rare surviving example of an urban working corn mill, powered by the River Itchen, which passes underneath it. It remained in use from 1743 until the early 20th century, and following a restoration project, is once more grinding flour. You can watch baking demonstrations in the mill, then take some freshly milled wholemeal flour to test your kneading skills at home. 🌐 nationaltrust.org.uk/winchester-city-mill

Walk 11

TEST WAY & CHILBOLTON COW COMMON

Distance: 5½ miles (8.8 km)

Map: OS Explorer 131 Romsey, Andover & Test Valley.
Grid ref: SU384389

How to get there: West Down Nature Reserve is 6 miles south of Andover, take the A3057/Romsey Road, pass The Mayfly's car park then the pub on your right. Go over the bridge and turn left, following the sign for the recycling centre, then almost instantly right again into the car park. **Sat nav:** SO20 6AX.

Parking: There is free parking at West Down Nature Reserve. Go to the recycling car park at the southern end of Coley Lane (there are two car parks for the reserve). Don't leave your car in the Mayfly car park as it is very small and usually full.

This fabulous walk takes in so many different habitats, including downland, chalk heath, woodland and water meadows, and showcases Hampshire countryside at its finest.

Railway enthusiasts will appreciate discovering the tracks of the old 'Sprat and Winkle Line' and Fullerton's former platform, still standing firm under a carpet of greenery. The path meanders past the rivers Test and Anton before leading you up Red Hill, with magnificent sweeping views across the valley. A winding path through copse and fields takes you to Chilbolton Cow Common, then through the picturesque village of Chilbolton with its many thatched cottages. The Abbots Mitre and the café in the village shop offer a welcome rest, before following the Test Way again through West Down Nature Reserve. There may be sheep in some fields and the common is grazed by cows.

THE PUB

THE MAYFLY has the perfect location with its waterside terrace and garden right on the banks of the River Test. It is often very busy and there's sometimes a wait for your food, but no one seems to mind spending a bit longer in such a superb setting. For winter walkers, the inside of the pub is cosy with beams and a wood burning stove. Opening times and menu for this Fuller's pub are on their website.

🌐 mayflyfullerton.co.uk ☎ 01264 860283

The Walk

1. From the car park, cross **Coley Lane** and turn left. Just before the bridge, turn right to follow the **Test Way** footpath. When you come to a junction, turn right following the sign to **Andover**. You are now following the former trackbed and as you cross the footbridge over the Test, look out for the railway sleepers that are still in place. Just after the bridge through the trees on the left are the remains of **Fullerton Junction** railway platform. Follow the track and pass the **Old Station House** on your left, then turn left at the information board.

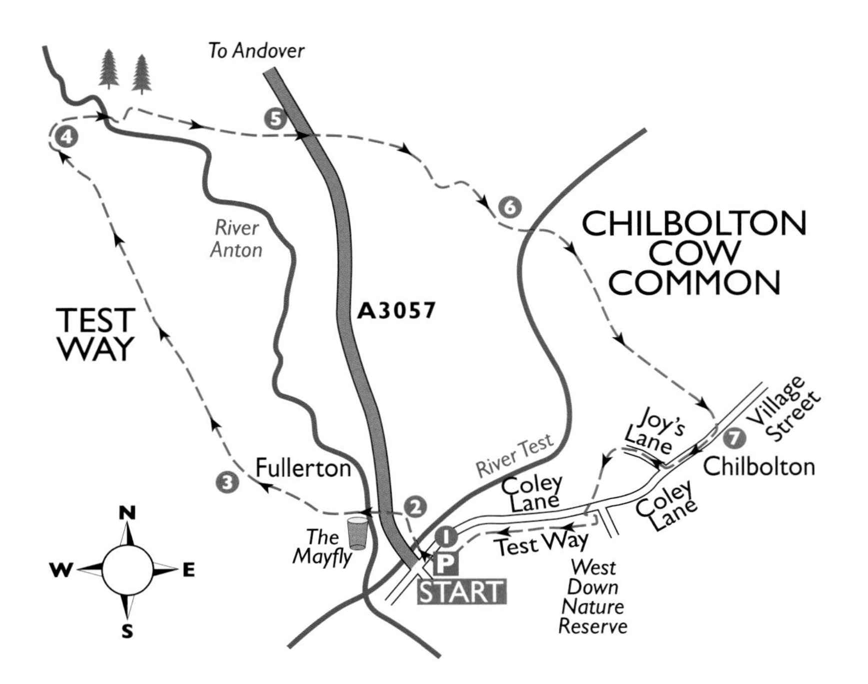

2 Now follow the track as it leads you under the A3057 and then left to **Fullerton Road**, again following the sign to Andover. Turn right at the road to cross the **River Anton**, and pass **Fullerton Mill**. Keep right at the junction, following the sign to **'Red Rise'**. Walk up the road and just past the village sign, when you get to **Fullerton Manor** on your left, turn right into the field.

3 Now turn left and follow the footpath across the top of the field. Stay in the same direction and eventually go through a metal kissing gate in front of you with a footpath arrow. Again stay in the same direction as you begin to head downhill. The path bears left, then at a path junction turn right and walk to a metal kissing gate.

4 Follow the footpath arrow over the bridge and continue, looking out for the River Anton on your left. There are often sheep in this field. Turn left through a gate and cross the footbridge. Now follow the path through trees to a junction where you turn right and walk by the side of a large field to a farm gate.

5 Go through the gate and cross the A3057 with care. Follow the gap in the hedge opposite then go through a gate. Now head diagonally right up a steep field. At the top, turn right and walk with the fence on your left and a wonderful view across the valley on your right. Go through a gate and continue ahead. Stay on this path with a hedge on your right until you come to the corner of a field. At the point where the hedge turns right, you turn left and head downhill, following the path between two fields.

6 At the bottom, turn left, taking the slightly higher grass path along the top of the bank for a short distance, then turn right and head down some steps to the road. Now turn left for about 50 metres, and then right to follow the **Test Way**. Go through the gate and cross long footbridges over the Test. Go through another gate into **Chilbolton Cow Common** and follow the path ahead. Cross a footbridge and turn sharp left. Go through a gate and follow the path, then go through another gate. Continue ahead through a series of gates, following the fence down to the road.

7 Turn right and follow **Village Street**, passing the **Abbots Mitre**, village shop and thatched cottages. Turn right at **Joy's Lane** to a car park and fork left. Now follow the Test Way as it leads you round a thatched cottage and just before the **Memorial Playing Field**, turn right and follow the path by a fence, through the trees. At the end of the fence turn left through a gate at the edge of the playing field and turn right, heading for another gate. Go through the gate and follow the path to **Coley Lane**. Cross the lane, turn left then right at the entrance to **West Down Nature Reserve**. Turn immediately right at the information board and go through a gate into the reserve. Follow the Test Way across the reserve, then the path leads downhill and you find yourself back at the car park.

Place of Interest Nearby

Longstock Park Water Garden covers around seven acres and opens on selected Sundays, from April to September, with donations to a nominated charity. Open daily are the farm shop, café, specialist plant nursery and garden emporium, making this the perfect spot for keen gardeners to stop awhile for some inspiration. 🌐 leckfordestate.co.uk

Walk 12
CHAWTON

Distance: 5 miles (8 km)

Map: OS Explorer OL33 Haslemere & Petersfield.
Grid ref: SU708375

How to get there: Chawton is in East Hampshire, just south of Alton, with the A31 skimming the edge of the village. **Sat nav:** GU34 1SB.

Parking: Free parking in Chawton village car park (turning next to Cassandra's Cup and the public car park is behind the pub car park).

Chawton is a delightful village, and the spot where Jane Austen spent the last eight years of her life. This walk on the edge of the South Downs National Park starts at Chawton. Then, an easy stretch of level walking through copse and by fields takes you to the equally idyllic village of Upper Farringdon, with thatched cottages, eccentric folly and a barn raised on staddle stones. Jane was a regular visitor to the village as she had friends in Farringdon, so you are truly walking in her footsteps. There has been a church here since the 12th century. There are a few stiles on this walk.

THE PUB

THE GREYFRIAR, with its beams and an open fire, is a relaxing, family and dog friendly spot to visit after a walk. It's conveniently sited directly opposite Jane Austen's house, with a garden and large car park. The menu offers larger meals as well as bar snacks and the service is prompt and friendly.

🌐 thegreyfriar.co.uk ☎ 01420 83841

The Walk

1. From the car park, turn left to return to the village street, with **Jane Austen's house** opposite and **Cassandra's Cup** tea room and **The Greyfriar** on your right. Turn left and follow the sign to **Chawton House**, passing a children's play area on your right. Look out for **Ferney Close** on your right, then cross the road and walk down this cul-de-sac. At the end on the left, follow the footpath, through a gate and along an enclosed path with fields either side. Cross a stile and down some steps to the A32.

2. Cross the road with care, then directly opposite go up the steps and through a gate. Now follow the path directly ahead, with arable fields either side. The path bears left through a copse before leaving the shade of the trees to follow the edge of fields, with sweeping views across the South Downs. Keep following the footpath arrows as you leave the fields to follow a track for about a mile, passing under an old bridge. When you see another bridge in front of you, turn right off the path to go up steps next to the bridge to a narrow lane. Turn left and walk back to the A32.

3. Cross again with care and follow the byway opposite, passing a sign on either side for **Manor Farm**. Follow the track until you come to a cross-track.

4. You are now at the edge of **Upper Farringdon**. Turn right and

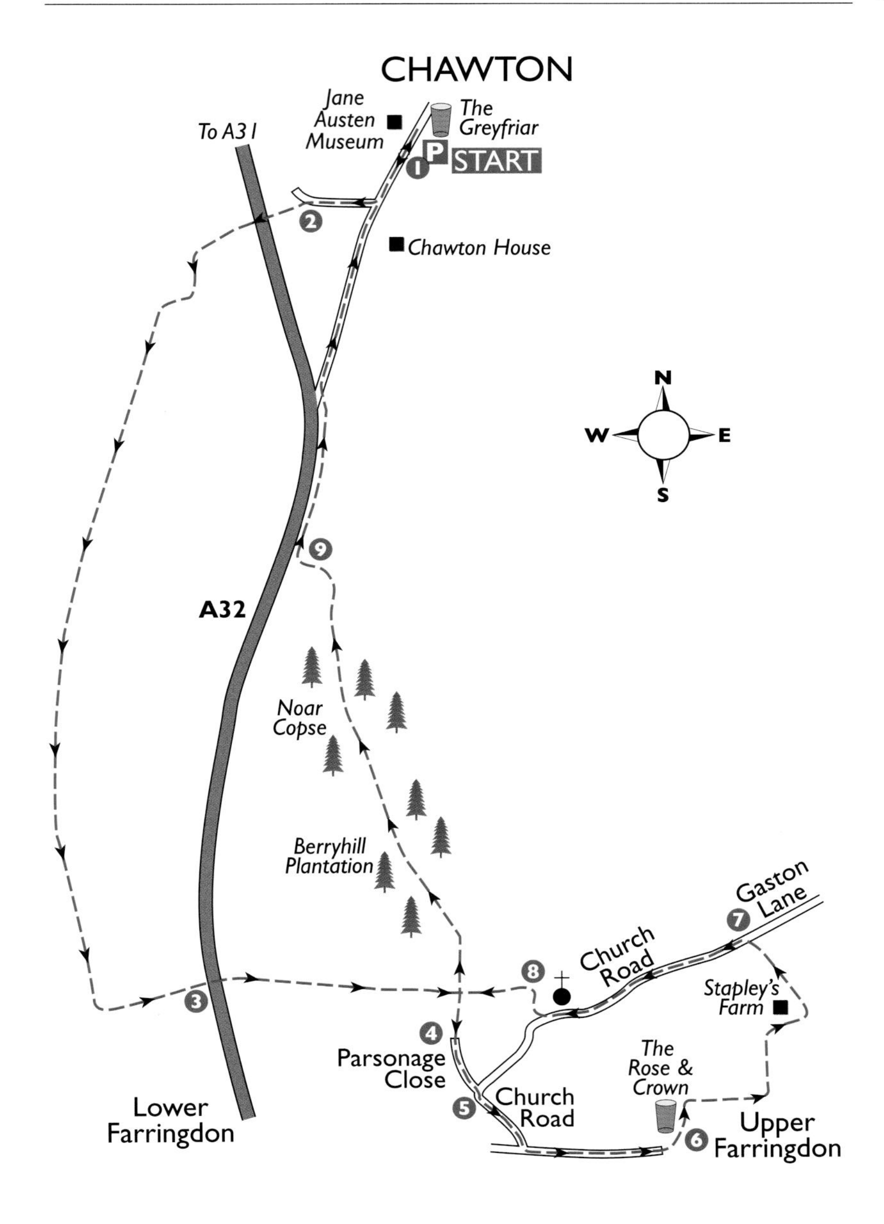

follow the footpath, walking between houses to **Parsonage Close**, follow the road down to a junction.

5 Cross the road and turn right to walk along the pavement of **Church Road** to a T-junction. Turn left along **The Street**, admiring the thatched cottages in this pretty village. At the end of the road, cross and follow the footpath directly ahead, with the garage of a thatched cottage on your right and the **Rose and Crown** on your left.

6 The footpath leads you into a field. Turn left then right to follow the edge of the field. Halfway along, where the path turns right, cross the stile on your left, then ahead across the field. At the field corner, turn right over a stile and head along a path to another stile to **Stapley's Farm**. Cross the farmyard then turn left along a track to a lane.

7 Turn left and walk along **Gaston Lane** to return to **Upper Farringdon**. Pass **Crows Lane** on your left and continue onto **Church Road** until you pass **All Saints' Church**, and **Massey's Folly** on the left. Turn right and follow the track with the church directly on your right, passing the sign for '**Northanger Benefice**' and walk up to a junction.

8 Turn left, passing the barn perched on staddle stones protecting the contents from mice, then keep ahead until you come to the path you walked down earlier at point 4. Now turn right up the track and through **Berryhill Plantation**, directly ahead across a field and through **Noar Copse**. Cross the stile then walk to the end of the field. Turn left to reach two stiles in the far corner by the A32.

9 Cross the stile on the right and follow the path with the A32 next to you. Cross another stile and continue straight on along the lane back into **Chawton**, passing **Chawton House** on your right, to return to your car.

Place of Interest Nearby

Jane Austen's House Museum in Chawton is the place where Jane Austen lived, wrote, revised and had published her major novels, including *Pride and Prejudice*. It is open seven days a week and holds various events throughout the year. 🌐 jane-austens-house-museum.org.uk. Jane also regularly walked down the lane to **Chawton House**, referred to as the 'Great House' in her letters. The house and gardens are open from March to December and **The Old Kitchen Tearoom** is a relaxing place to rest after a good walk. 🌐 chawtonhouse.org

Walk 13
SELBORNE

Distance: 5½ miles (8.8 km)

Map: OS Explorer OL33 Haslemere & Petersfield.
Grid ref: SU742335

How to get there: Selborne is 15 miles south of Basingstoke along the A339, then take the B3006 into the village. **Sat nav:** GU34 3JR.

Parking: Free public car park behind the Selborne Arms in the middle of the High Street, and also in the middle of this walk.

The National Trust look after 267 acres of countryside around Selborne, on the edge of the South Downs National Park. This figure-of-eight walk starts in the village with a 3-mile walk north-east to explore the valley meadows and woodlands of the Lythes, then up to Selborne Common for a 2½-mile loop exploring its magnificent trees and sunny glades. The village High Street is lined with thatched cottages and with a delightful village shop, tearoom and the fascinating museum, this is a wonderful place to spend the day. The walk through the Lythes follows a section of the Hangers Way, a long-distance footpath named after the steep-sided wooded hills known as 'Hangers' that are a feature of this landscape.

THE PUB

THE SELBORNE ARMS is a charming traditional pub with a large open fire. It features five local real ales and for summer days there is a play area in the garden behind the pub, as well as a wishing well barbecue. It serves locally sourced food daily. Dogs are not allowed in the pub.
selbornearms.co.uk ☎01420 511247

The Walk

1. From the car park, walk down to the **High Street** and turn left. Just past the **Gilbert White and Oates Museum**, cross the road and take the entrance into Selborne churchyard to the right of the war memorial. There is a sign leading you to Gilbert White's grave if you want to look for it. Walk down to the bottom right corner and through a swing gate into **Church Meadow**.

2. Now walk straight down to a wooden bridge across the stream. Cross and pass a National Trust sign for the **Short Lythe**, passing steep banks of beech and ash. Continue straight on following the green arrows, then through two wooden swing gates into the **Long Lythe**.

3. Pass a small iron bench on your left, with meadows sweeping down on your right, often grazed by cattle, and beech woods on your left. Go through a gate at the other side of the **Lythe** into a large field with ponds.

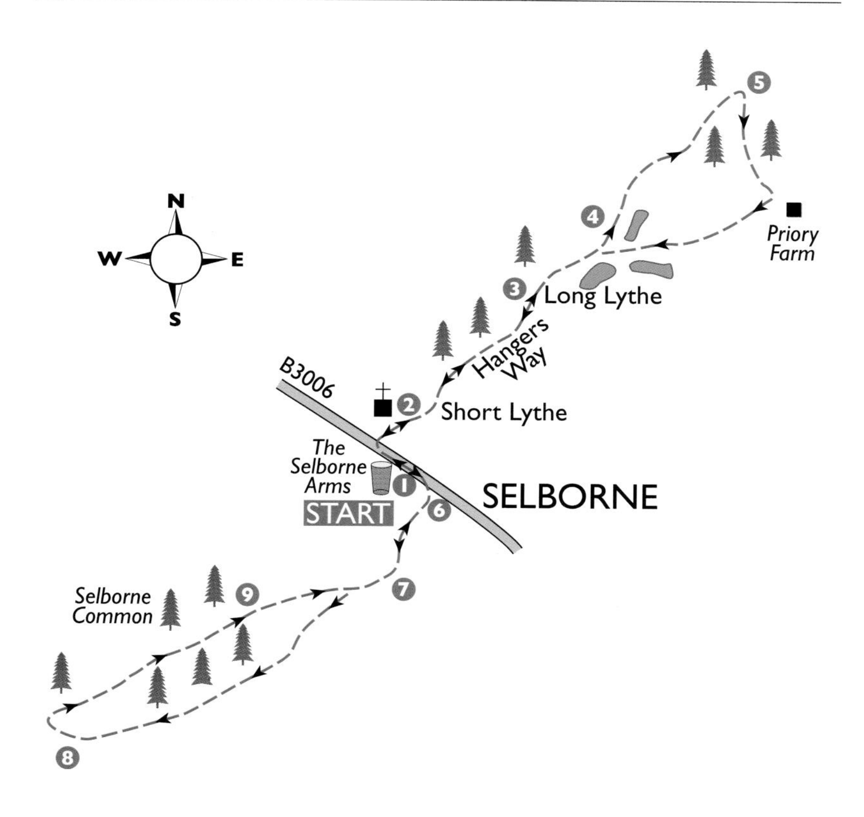

4 Follow the public footpath towards **Wick Wood**, where the path passes to the right of the water and through a swing gate. Head up the field, following the **Hangers Way** and turn right through a gate and stile into woods. This shady path leads you across a field and over a stile by a gate to a wide cross track.

5 Turn right and follow the path through the trees towards **Priory Farm**. Just before the farm, there are metal swing gates on either side of the path. Go through the gate on your right and follow the footpath across the field, then through a swing gate on your right into woods. This path leads you back to the footbridge at point 2. Cross the bridge and retrace your steps across the **Lythes** and through the churchyard, then turn left along the **High Street** to return to the car park and the second loop of the walk.

6 Follow the signed public footpath at the bottom of the car park, leading up to the **Zig-Zag** and **Selborne Common**. Go through the footpath gate to the bottom of the Zig-Zag path. If you need a rest there are iron seats along the way with excellent views over **Selborne** and the **Oakhanger woods**.

7 At the top, head right and uphill to go through a gate on to **Selborne Common**. Turn immediately left to follow a grassy path. Stay on this route until you come to a fingerpost in the far bottom corner of the Common.

8 Now turn right then almost immediately right again by a second fingerpost – there are two paths, take the one on the right. Head up a wide track back towards the Common.

9 Pass **The Green**, a wide grassy area on your left. Keep in the same direction along **The Pipeline** – a wide grassy path, until you come back to the gate at the top of the Zig-Zag. Then retrace your steps back down to the car.

Place of Interest Nearby

The 18th-century naturalist Gilbert White made exploring the flora and fauna of the surrounding beech woods and flower-filled meadows his life study. His book *The Natural History and Antiquities of Selborne* was first published in 1789 and has been continuously in print ever since, making it the fourth most published book in the English language. The house where he lived is now the **Gilbert White's House and Gardens Museum**. Children will marvel at the stuffed animals and tiny bat skeletons, while 30 acres of gardens will appeal to the adults. There are also galleries covering the lives of the Victorian explorer Frank Oates and his nephew Lawrence 'Titus' Oates, who with gangrene and frostbite walked out of a tent into the Antarctic blizzard to improve the chances of survival of his three companions, on Scott's doomed South Pole expedition in 1912. There are also sleds and wolfskin mittens to explore in a reconstructed rondavel house. 🌐 gilbertwhiteshouse.org.uk

Walk 14
Old Basing

Distance: 4½ miles (7.2 km)

Map: OS Explorer 144 Basingstoke, Alton & Whitchurch.
Grid ref: SU660530

How to get there: From the M3, take exit 6 onto the A339, then follow Redbridge Lane to Barton's Lane and follow the brown signs to Basing House car park. **Sat nav:** RG24 8AE.

Parking: Basing House car park, off Barton's Lane and just past Barton's Mill pub.

A few minutes from Basingstoke town centre lies Old Basing, with its thatched cottages, red brick houses and the ruins of the largest private dwelling in Tudor England, Basing House. The walk starts at a riverside pub and explores wide open spaces at Millfield Nature Reserve, Basingstoke Common and Crabtree Plantation – with woods, views and wildlife all just a stone's throw from the town centre. Stop awhile to explore the historic ruins of Basing House, before crossing the Loddon to return to the pub. Its unfortunate occupants picked the losing side during the English Civil War in the 1640s, and subsequently suffered at the hands of Oliver Cromwell who burnt this magnificent house to the ground. However, the Tudor Great Barn still stands, and although battle scarred, it has managed to survive the tests of time almost unscathed.

THE PUB

BARTON'S MILL is a converted mill by the banks of the River Loddon, with the remnants of a working waterwheel by the large pub garden. It serves seasonal food with gluten-free options, as well as real English ales and superb gins.

bartonsmillpubanddining.co.uk ☎ 01256 331153

The Walk

1. Leave the car park, passing **Barton's Mill** on your right, and go straight ahead into **Millfield Nature Reserve**. Now follow the path across the large meadow, passing under electricity pylons and heading for its northern tip. Look out for the odd green arrow marking the '**Basing Trail**' as you walk.

2. When you are almost at the top of the nature reserve, there's a post and a gap in the hedge on the left. Turn down the path for about 10 metres, then turn right to follow the footpath to **Bartons Lane**. Walk up the road, then right at the corner to walk down **Pyotts Hill**, crossing a small bridge over the **River Loddon** as you head for a road junction.

3. At the junction, cross with care and walk through the small car park to the right of the village hall. Take the footpath across **Oliver's Battery**, heading roughly south. This was once the site of a motte and bailey castle. Cross a small footbridge to an information board and old red phone box, now used for swapping books.

4. If you have a dog, to avoid walking past the cricket club (which has a 'No Dogs' sign, turn right and walk up the lane, then left down **The Street**, and left again down **Riley Lane**. If no dog, turn left and walk down the lane, passing the bowling club, then follow the footpath past the cricket club and a children's play area to go through a gate. Turn left down Riley Lane. Pass allotments on one side and **Old Basing Lawn Tennis Club** on the other. Continue to the bottom of the lane, walking under beech and oak trees to the railway, then cross the footbridge over the track.

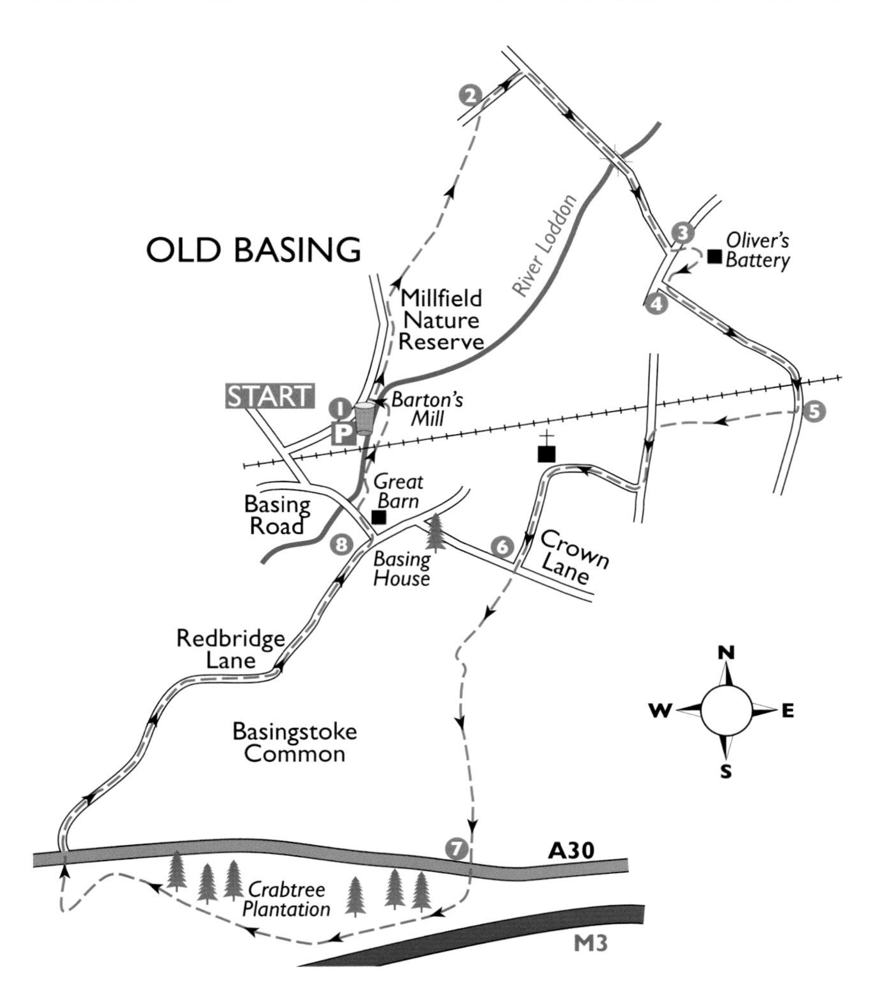

5 Turn right and follow the shady footpath under the trees to **Milkingpen Lane**. Cross the road and turn left, following the pavement past some pretty cottages, then turn right down **Church Lane**, opposite the school. Follow this lane, passing more cottages, then go through the wooden gate into the churchyard of **St Mary's**. Follow the path through the churchyard, with the church on your right. You come back out onto **Church Lane** (which loops round the churchyard). Turn left and follow the lane a short distance to a bend, then go straight on, following a shady footpath, passing a cemetery on your left, until you come to **Crown Lane**.

6 Cross the road and walk through the car park to a swing gate. Now head south across **Basingstoke Common**, ignoring any side paths and walking under the power lines, to a metal swing gate and sign for **Basingstoke Canal Heritage Path**.

7 Go through the gate, and cross the A30 with care to walk under **Bolton Arch** into **Crabtree Plantation**. The footpath skirts the trees, heading west, with the A30 on your right, on the other side of the trees. The path leads down to a play area, then turns right for about 20 metres to the road. Cross back again with care (there is an island in the middle of the road for pedestrians). Then walk up **Redbridge Lane** – there is another play area on your right here near the car park.

8 The road ends at a junction, by the red brick walls of **Basing House**. You can either turn left down **Basing Road**, then right just before the bridge to follow the riverside footpath to the pub. Alternatively, walk a few metres down **The Street**, then turn left through a wooden gate to see the stunning barn, and through the **Basing House visitor centre** (which sells ice creams) following the footpath down to the river. Turn right and follow the river back to the pub and car park.

Place of Interest Nearby

The Vyne is a former Tudor palace, once visited by Henry VIII and the unfortunate Anne Boleyn, and is just 4 miles north of Basingstoke. The house is managed by the National Trust, and for birdwatchers there are purpose-built bird hides offering panoramic views across the wetlands. The Brewhouse Tea Room offers indoor and outdoor seating and dogs are welcome on a lead in the gardens and woods. 🌐 nationaltrust.org.uk/the-vyne

Walk 15

WHITCHURCH WATERMILLS

Distance: 5½ miles (8.8 km)

Map: OS Explorer 144 Basingstoke, Alton & Whitchurch.
Grid ref: SU462481

How to get there: Whitchurch is halfway between Winchester and Newbury and 4 miles off the A34. There is a roundabout in the centre of the small village, with the White Hart on the corner, or for the Winchester Road car park follow the signs to the Silk Mill. **Sat nav:** RG28 7DN (The White Hart) Winchester Road car park (RG28 7HP).

Parking: The White Hart has a small pub car park. Alternatively, park on London Street, just past the pub where there is free roadside parking on weekends, or in the free Winchester Road car park at point 2 of the walk.

This walk follows the River Test, across the North Wessex Downs between the villages of Whitchurch and Laverstoke. This beautiful clear chalk stream is well stocked with large trout and is best admired from the bridge in Whitchurch. Most of the river is now privately owned and carefully fenced off for fishing rights, but there is the odd spot along this walk where you can see the water.

The walk continues across the meadows to Laverstoke, home of the Bombay Sapphire Distillery, housed in a former paper mill. Mills are a feature of this walk, which shows the role the river played in this area's industry, as you pass Bere Mill, Town Mill and the Silk Mill.

THE PUB

THE WHITE HART is a popular village pub, with a restaurant, bar and outside seating area. It dates back to the mid-15th century, with 600 years' history of serving drinks to the people of Whitchurch. You can choose to sit in the bar or dining room and this Arkell's pub serves modern and traditional pub food, sandwiches and a takeaway menu, with dogs and walkers both welcome. 🌐 whitehartotelwhitchurch.co.uk ☎ 01256 892900

The Walk

1. From the **White Hart**, walk down to the roundabout in the centre of **Whitchurch** and turn left down **Winchester Street**. Cross the bridge of the **Mill Race**, a branch of the **Test** diverted to power the watermill. A little further on you pass the **Silk Mill** on your right, then cross a bridge over the Test. It's worth stopping to see the large trout hovering in the water below you.

2. Now directly opposite the **Winchester Road car park**, turn left to follow a narrow footpath. At the end of this path, veer to the right into a small recreation ground, then follow the concrete footpath ahead to the road. Turn left and walk down **McFauld Way**, then at the bend, continue ahead along the footpath, which skirts the edge of the primary school grounds. When you come to the metal school gate, turn left, passing **Town Mill**, then almost immediately right – don't cross the bridge. Now follow a shady path under the trees, with the Test fenced off on your left.

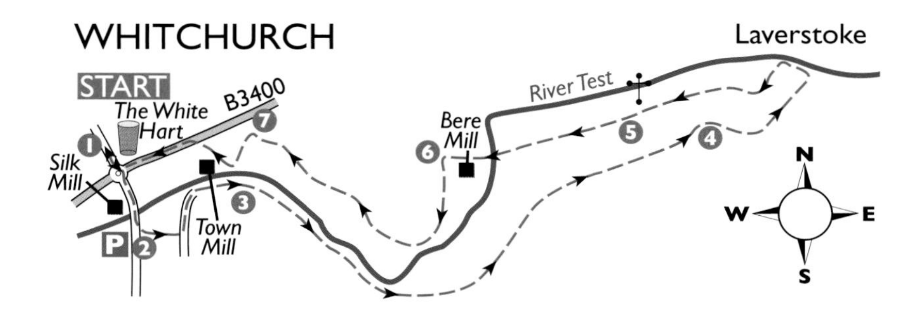

❸ Keep to this path by the Test, if the nettles are too long, there is another parallel path that is more open. At 1.2 miles into the walk, just as the path leads uphill, turn left down a short path to a kissing gate. Through the gate follow the path ahead, towards a hanger of trees. Go through another gate signed '**Mill Trail**' then walk by the side of the trees with lovely sweeping views to your left. Another gate takes you to a hill, which you walk up for a sweeping view across the valley, with **Bere Mill** below you on your left – look out for their rare breed cattle as you walk. There is a kissing gate in the top right corner with a Mill Trail sign. Go through the gate and walk with a field on your left.

❹ At a T-junction, turn right to follow the footpath sign under the trees. The path leads you downhill into the village of **Laverstoke**. Turn left and walk past pretty, former estate cottages. At the end of this road is **Bombay Sapphire**, which is worth the short detour to have a look at, even if you aren't ready for a gin. The footpath is next to the Bombay Sapphire car park. Follow the narrow path down some steps, then veer left as the path leads you past the field of **Overton Black Arrows**, then tennis courts. At the corner of the tennis court, look out for a footpath sign on your right. Go through the metal gate then head off directly ahead across the meadow. Look out for the 13th-century **St Nicholas Church** in **Freefolk** on your right, with its distinctive weatherboarded bellcote and pyramidal roof.

❺ At the corner of the field is an impressive sycamore by a wooden kissing gate. Go through the gate and follow the footpath arrow to cross the track and straight on through another kissing gate to follow the footpath ahead. You can catch the odd glimpse of the River Test at the bottom of the hill. At the end of the field, go through a wooden swing gate and walk down to cross the red brick bridge, stopping to admire **Bere Mill** on your left.

6 Walk ahead along a surfaced drive and when you come to a wooden farm gate with a swing gate next to it, turn left through the gate, again following the footpath sign. Walk up the side of a large field, then through a swing gate to follow the side of a field, with the Test on your left through the trees. Stay on this path as it narrows and leads you back to Whitchurch – there can be nettles here in summer.

7 When you get to Whitchurch, walk ahead along a surfaced path, then turn left down **The Green** for a few metres, and just before the sign for **Pound Meadow**, turn left down a footpath. Cross two footbridges to **Town Mill**. It's worth standing on the bridge for a view of the Test, but to continue the walk go in the opposite direction, and walk down **Town Mill Lane**, passing **Town Mill Cottage**. Cross a bridge over **Mill Stream** and you find yourself back on **London Street**. Turn left and pass **The Red House**, then continue down the road to **The White Hart**.

Places of Interest Nearby

Whitchurch Silk Mill is the oldest silk mill in the UK, still in its original building. It is a Georgian watermill that weaves silk using 19th-century machinery. You can see the original mill wheel still in operation, admire the fabrics on the looms, then be tempted by the silk products in the shop, with a tearoom by the banks of the Test. It is open year round and holds a changing programme of exhibitions. 🌐 whitchurchsilkmill.org.uk

Bombay Sapphire gin is made at Laverstoke Mill, and visitors can have a tour of the distillery, including visiting the glasshouses where the plants used as botanicals in the production of Bombay Sapphire gin are grown. There is a beautiful bar where you can relax and enjoy a gin cocktail. 🌐 bombaysapphire.com

Walk 16

Overton to Steventon

Distance: 7¾ miles (12.4 km)

Map: OS Explorer 144 Basingstoke, Alton & Whitchurch.
Grid ref: SU515496

How to get there: Overton lies between Andover and Basingstoke. From the A34, take the turning for Whitchurch, then follow the B3400 through Whitchurch, Laverstock and into Overton. Go straight over at the crossroads, with the White Hart on the corner, to find the car park. **Sat nav:** RG25 3NP.

Parking: Free car park on London Road, just past the White Hart on the right. There is another car park just further along on the left if it's full.

Overton is the largest village in Hampshire, with signs of Stone Age, Bronze Age and Celtic occupation from archaeological finds and barrows nearby. This charming village is a good starting point with pubs and shops for picnics and provisions for the walk. An easy, mainly level walk crossing fields once walked by a young Jane Austen to the village she grew up in. Visit the 12th-century church where her father was rector, then return with sweeping views across Ashe Park. Walk through picturesque Ashe village, by the source of the River Test, with gorgeous cottages and a village orchard to return to Overton and a well-deserved drink in a friendly pub. Some of the fields on the way to Steventon have sheep and there's one stile.

THE PUB

THE WHITE HART has recently been refurbished and is filled with charm and character. This is a lovely friendly pub and very dog friendly. Inside, there's a mix of antiques, reclaimed fittings and artwork creating a delightful space to sit and relax after a long walk. There is a decked outside seating area for sunny days. 🌐 whitehartoverton.co.uk ☎ 01256 771431

The Walk

❶ From the **White Hart** pub, cross the road and head south down **Winchester Street**. Follow the road right through the village, then turn left along **Pound Road**. Head uphill, then turn right down **Waltham Road**. Walk past houses, then just as you go round a corner turn left at a wooden footpath sign with a handrail.

❷ Follow the path towards **Berrydown Farm**. Go through the gate then turn right, following the tarmac track past cow sheds. As the track veers to the left, go through a farm gate, following the footpath arrow. Stay on this surfaced track as you follow the edge of **Berrydown Copse**.

❸ When you get to the point where the track veers to the right, leave the track and turn sharp left to follow the wide grassy path, still with the copse on your left. This path skirts the edge of the trees to a metal kissing gate on your left, again signed with a footpath arrow. Go through this gate, then another gate a few

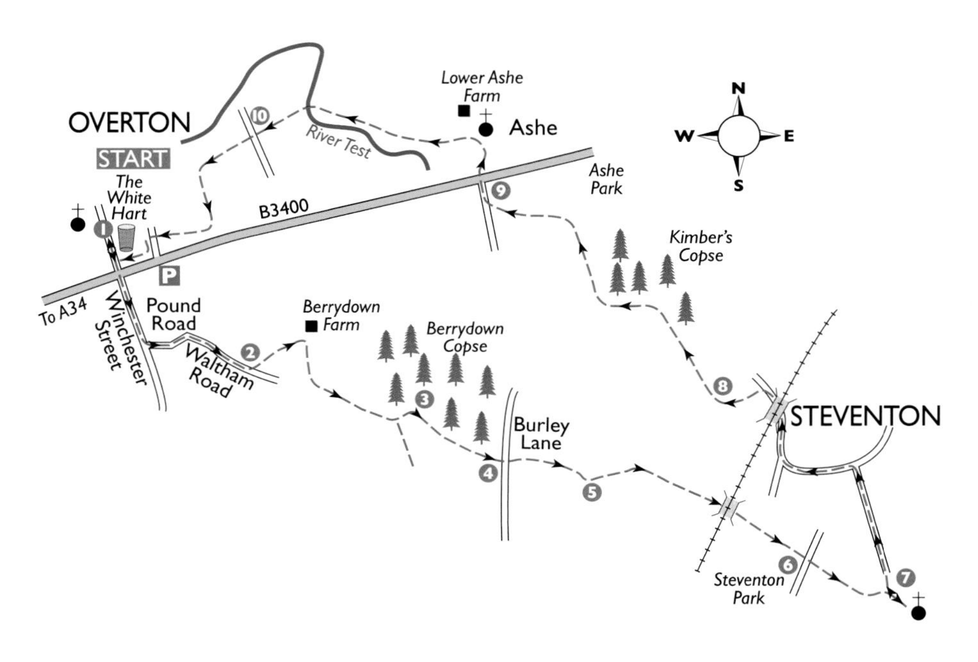

metres along into a field. The footpath isn't clear, but head left up the hill towards the trees.

4 At the top of the field, go through a metal kissing gate, cross the narrow road, and follow the narrow footpath directly opposite, passing gardens on your left to a kissing gate. The next few fields might have sheep so if you have a dog make sure it is on a lead. The footpath leads you straight across the field to a metal kissing gate in the hedge. After about 10 metres, go through the kissing gate on your right and you are now on a track.

5 Turn left and follow the track to the corner. Now turn right, leaving the track to follow a narrow grassy path, passing by the side of a farm gate, with a fence on your left and a hedge on your right. You come to a railway tunnel that takes you under the tracks. Then head towards the houses as you approach **Steventon**.

6 Cross the road and go straight on, following the footpath sign.

You are now walking across **Steventon Park**, with an arable field on your left and hedgerow on your right. At the metal gate, turn left and follow the footpath until you come to another gate. Go through the gate and the church is on your right, and well worth a quick detour to visit.

7 To continue the walk, turn left and follow the lane to a curved road on the edge of Steventon. Turn left and walk to a small triangular green with a tree and bench. Head right, passing the **Jane Austen telephone box book exchange and information centre**. Go back under the railway, pass a long drive on your left then turn left to follow the footpath sign, through a gate.

8 Head up the side of a field, through a gate then up some steps to another gate. Cross the next field, heading uphill then through another gate. Turn right following the footpath and head into **Kimber's Copse**. Stay on the main path, ignoring a left then right turn. You soon leave the trees to walk by the side of a field with sweeping views to your right across the parkland. The footpath leads you down to a wooden kissing gate. Go through the gate and turn right. Walk down the field towards some houses, but before you get there, turn left to follow the footpath across the field and through a metal kissing gate. Now head diagonally across the corner of a field to another gate on your right. Go through the gate, turn left then through another gate to **Burley Lane.**

9 Turn right and walk up the lane to the busy B3400. Cross with care, then head straight on into **Ashe**. Go through the lychgate of the church into the churchyard. Pass the church and take the gate in the left corner. Turn right and walk towards the farm. The footpath is signed with a left then right turn. Go through a wooden kissing gate and straight on. Cross the stile (with a dog gate) and over a small footbridge. Don't turn direct left, instead veer left but also uphill, across an arable field.

10 Cross **Berrydown Lane**, then through a gap in the hedge and straight on following the field edge until you come to the edge of **Overton Recreation Centre**, with **St Mary's Church** visible on your right. Turn right, walk under the telegraph wires, and pass

some mosaic benches on your left as you walk downhill, now with the church ahead. Cross a road and follow the footpath ahead, passing **Overton Hill playground**. Walk through a small car park to the road and turn right to return to the pub.

Place of Interest Nearby

Jane Austen was born in **Steventon** and lived there from 1775 to 1801, when she moved to Bath with her parents. Sadly, the rectory where she lived was pulled down, with the site marked by an old lime tree planted by her eldest brother, James. But the church where her father was rector remains unchanged and inside you can find memorial tablets to various members of the Austen family. A touching tribute to the author is a red telephone box in the centre of the village, which has been converted into a Jane Austen information centre and book exchange.

Walk 17

WATERSHIP DOWN

Distance: 7½ miles (12 km)

Map: OS Explorer 144 Basingstoke, Alton & Whitchurch.
Grid ref: SU499595

How to get there: Ecchinswell lies between the A34 and the A339, north-west of Basingstoke. The pub is on the main Ecchinswell Road, in the centre of the village. **Sat nav:** RG20 4UH.

Parking: The Royal Oak car park in Ecchinswell.

An exhilarating walk on the North Wessex Downs with breathtaking views across the downland made famous by former local resident Richard Adams' book, *Watership Down*. The route passes Nuthanger Farm, also mentioned in the novel. Andrew Lloyd Webber is another local resident, owning Sydmonton Court. He founded Watership Down Stud, and this walk passes right by its immaculate stables and elegant racehorses. You also pass Ladle Hill, the site of a rare 'unfinished' Iron Age hillfort, on the site of an earlier Bronze Age settlement. The sloping chalky grassland supports many rare plant species, including orchids, and this walk is perfect for spotting butterflies on long summer days. Dog walkers be aware there are sheep.

THE PUB

THE ROYAL OAK is a relaxed pub with a very large beer garden behind. The menu offers good food at a reasonable price, with excellent baguette sandwiches on a Sunday if you don't fancy a roast.
🌐 royaloakecchinswell.co.uk
☎ 01635 297355

The Walk

1 With your back to the pub, turn right and walk up **Ecchinswell Road** a short distance to **Mill Lane**. Turn right and follow this pretty lane past **The Old School House** and a stream. Continue ahead as it turns into a track, then go through the gate on your right between fields. Go through a gap at the end of this path then turn right by the side of a large field. Cross a stile and over the next field, then another stile to a road.

2 Turn left and walk by the side of the road for about 50 metres to a footpath sign on your right. Follow the path by a hedgerow heading slightly uphill. The path winds past hedges to a wood as you steadily head uphill. At a cross track turn left to follow a surfaced drive with **Watership Down** ahead of you.

3 At the road, turn right and walk downhill to the crossroads, then turn left following the sign to **Ashley Warren**. Follow the road which leads you uphill, with wonderful views across the valley on your right.

4 At the top of the hill, detour to the top of Watership Down by crossing the road then turn left to follow a narrow path uphill for about 10 minutes to the **Gallops** on top of Watership Down and a magnificent view. Then retrace your steps to the road.

5 Cross the road and go through the gate to follow the **Wayfarer's Walk**, with a row of tall trees on your right. If you have a dog it is best they are on a lead here as there are normally sheep. Shortly you come to a gate on your right signed **Sydmonton Court Estate**. Go through the gate and walk across the ridge of

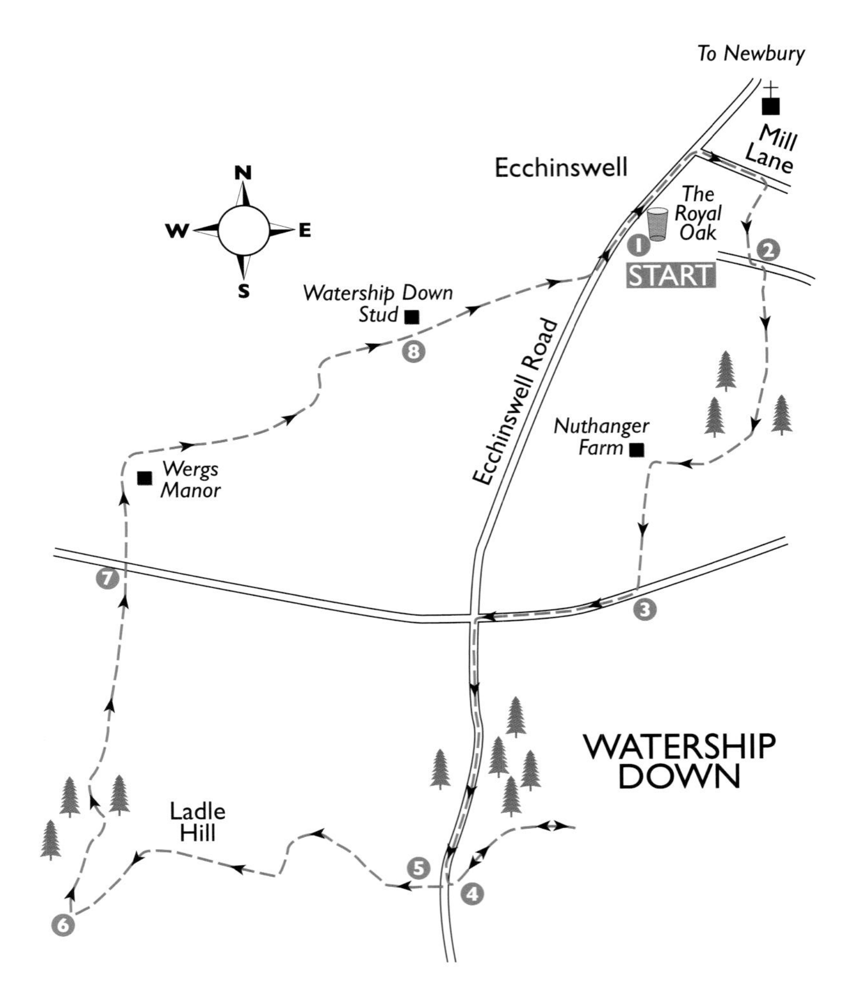

the hill to a gate. Now turn left to walk by the side of an arable field. The path veers right across the centre of the field, passing a bell barrow on your right – a Bronze Age tomb chamber. You then reach the summit of **Ladle Hill** with the path following the edge of the Iron Age hillfort before veering to the left.

6 When you come to a path on your right, leave the Wayfarer's Walk and follow this new path, heading north. Walk through woods and continue straight on until you come to a road.

7 Cross straight over the road and continue in the same direction, following the sign to **Burghclere**. Pass **Wergs Manor** on your right then turn right by a brick wall to follow the footpath. The path ends at a cross track by an oak tree, where you turn left. When you see **Laundry Cottages** ahead, look out for a path on your right that leads you between the fields.

8 At **Watership Down Stud**, follow the footpath to the right of the stables, then at the road, turn left to return to the pub.

Place of Interest Nearby

The novel, ***Watership Down***, tells the story of a group of rabbits forced to migrate to the Hampshire Downs to escape the destruction of their warren. It was Adams' first novel, and was never originally intended for publication. He told the story to his two daughters to keep them entertained over a long car journey, with the story developing over three weeks of school runs. His daughters were then so enthralled by the tale that they wanted a permanent copy and so he wrote his first novel. The manuscript was turned down by 12 publishers, before an independent publisher spotted its potential, with it becoming an instant bestseller. Richard Adams was born in 1920 in nearby Wash Common, Newbury, and lived in Whitchurch, celebrating his 90th birthday in The White Hart. He died in 2016, aged 96.

Walk 18
BURGHCLERE

Distance: 5 miles (8km)

Map: OS Explorer 158 Newbury & Hungerford and OS Explorer 144 Basingstoke, Alton & Whitchurch. **Grid ref:** SU462607

How to get there: Burghclere is ½ mile east of the A34, with brown tourist signs for Sandham Memorial Chapel making it easy to locate. Take the Tot Hill exit and follow the signs to Burghclere. Drive through the village, and the car park and pub are next to each other on Harts Lane. **Sat nav:** RG20 9JT.

Parking: There is a free National Trust car park, next to The Carpenters Arms and opposite Sandham Memorial Chapel. Keep an eye on the time though, as the gate is locked 15 minutes after the chapel closes. If the pub is quiet you could park in its small car park.

Easy walking across fields and byways south of the small village of Burghclere, with pastoral views across the North Wessex Downs towards Watership Down. You also pass through the grounds of Earlstone Manor, a Grade II listed manor house dating back to the 1300s. The walk starts opposite Sandham Memorial Chapel, which houses dramatic murals of the First World War, by Stanley Spencer. There are stiles on the walk, but all with dog gates, making this a good dog walk with plenty of opportunities for your hound to be off-lead. The walk is mainly level, with a shady stretch of boardwalk through The Alders woodland in the middle.

THE PUB

THE CARPENTERS ARMS is a friendly, traditional pub with a garden behind offering excellent views across Watership Down, popular with walkers and locals. It's owned by Arkell's brewers and serves a range of hand-crafted beers. Dogs are welcome in the bar.

carpentersarms-burghclere.co.uk ☎ 01635 278251

The Walk

1. With your back to the **Carpenters Arms**, turn left and walk down **Harts Lane** towards the A34. Beside **Holmbush Cottage**, the last house in the village, turn left and follow the lane for about 200 metres, passing **Ashold Farm**.

2. Just before a sharp bend to the right, leave the lane to follow the footpath sign on your right, marked with a yellow arrow. An enclosed path leads to a stile, then follow the field path ahead. Pass **Budd's Farm** on the left and veer left to follow the edge of the farm's garden, through a gap in the fence and under a large tree (don't go ahead over the stile). Then head across the edge of the field to a stile, with a yellow footpath arrow.

3. Turn right and follow the footpath between the trees. You come to another stile in the corner of a large field. Walk ahead a few metres, then veer left, following the grass path to a clear cross path in the middle of the field. Now turn right and head towards the trees. Follow the narrow boardwalk through **The Alders**. When the boardwalk ends, keep ahead on the path, passing holly bushes until you come to a field.

4. Turn sharp right and walk a short distance to the corner of the field. Turn right again to cross a plank footbridge over a small stream. Go through a gate into a field and head for the farm building you can see ahead of you, admiring the view on your left as you walk. At the other side, head for the gate with the barn on your right and a large pond on your left.

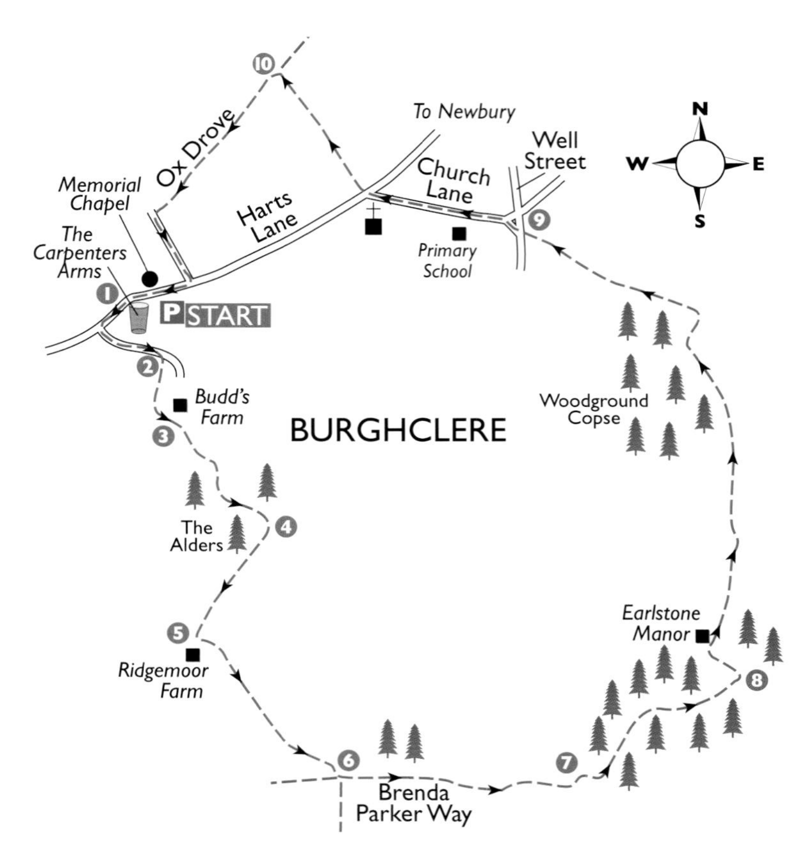

5 Go through the gate with **Ridgemoor Farm** opposite you. Turn left and follow the byway along a hedge-lined track, passing arable fields.

6 Eventually you come to a cross-track where you turn left uphill on the **Brenda Parker Way**. Walk past trees, then the path starts to head downhill until you come to a narrow road.

7 Turn left in 20 metres where you will come to a junction, then turn right and walk uphill, following the sign to **Ecchinswell and Kingsclere**. After about another 10 metres, and just before another junction, turn left off the road to follow a bridleway through a band of trees.

8 The path emerges from the trees at a cross track, with a field on either side of you, a few metres gap then more hedge. If you look in the field on your left you will spot some large gates with brick gate posts, over to the right on the opposite side of the field. These are the gates to **Earlstone Manor**. Turn left and walk across the field, then right to the gates, keeping a stream on your left. There is a small gate next to the gates with a blue footpath arrow. Go through the gate and follow the path past the manor house and through its grounds. Stay on this main track as you pass a pond and another house, ignoring a footpath leading off to the right. Go through a gate and take the main path that veers off to the left, following the blue arrow, ignoring a path that leads off on the right. Now stay on this ridged track for a long stretch as it leads you past **Woodground Copse** and back towards **Burghclere**.

9 Eventually you come to a crossroads by a house. Cross **Well Street** and go straight ahead along **Church Lane**, following the sign for **Sandham Memorial Chapel**. Pass the village primary school, then the church, to come to a junction with a war memorial. Cross straight over **Harts Lane** to follow the footpath sign ahead, along a narrow path past houses and a holly hedge, then fields and fence. At the end of the path, go through a kissing gate, to continue across a field to another gate.

10 Turn left along **Ox Drove**, passing blackberry bushes, then continue straight on as it turns into a surfaced lane with houses on your left. At the junction, turn left down **Pound Lane**, then right along **Harts Lane**. Cross a bridge over the old railway track to return to Sandham Memorial Chapel, the car park and pub.

Place of Interest Nearby

Inside the 1920s **Sandham Memorial Chapel** are paintings by Stanley Spencer, depicting his experiences during the First World War. He was born in Cookham, in 1891, and attended the Slade School of Fine Art. He enlisted in the Royal Army Medical Corps, then transferred to the Infantry and went to the Front Line in 1917. The war had a profound effect on him and the murals are considered to be one of the greatest of all war memorials.
nationaltrust.org.uk/sandham-memorial-chapel

Walk 19
FACCOMBE

Distance: 3 miles (4.8 km)

Map: OS Explorer 131Romsey, Andover & Test Valley.
Grid ref: SU391579

How to get there: Faccombe is 8 miles north of Andover, off the A343. Turn off the A343 by the Yew Tree Inn (a pub also worth visiting), follow the road through Ashmansworth, then along a single track to Faccombe. The Jack Russell Inn is signed on your left. **Sat nav:** SP11 0DS.

Parking: The Jack Russell Inn has a large car park.

Faccombe is tucked away in the North Downs and is blessed with an abundance of clearly marked footpaths, making this a very popular spot for walkers and cyclists. Much of the land is owned by the Faccombe Estate and is used for shooting between September and February, so don't be surprised if you see lots of partridge and pheasants in the woods. There are attractive tree-lined avenues in the surrounding parkland by the village, while the chalk downland is known as the breadbasket of southern England. This walk takes you past fields of wheat with distant views over the rolling landscape, as well as woods filled with bluebells in spring.

THE PUB

THE JACK RUSSELL INN is exactly what you would want at the end of the walk. There is plenty of space in this tastefully decorated, dog friendly pub, with a cosy fire for winter walkers, or tables outside, looking out over the village pond, for summer days.

🌐 thejackrussellinn.com ☎ 01264 737315.

If you would prefer afternoon tea, **The Tea Cosy** in nearby Hurstbourne Tarrant is a delightful independent café with the most amazing cakes.

🌐 theteacosyhampshire.com ☎ 01264 736644

The Walk

1. With your back to the pub, turn left and walk to the main road, then turn right to the junction. Now turn left and walk with the brick and flint wall of **Faccombe Manor** on your left, following the narrow road to **Ashmansworth**.

2. Look out for double farm gates on your left and a footpath sign.

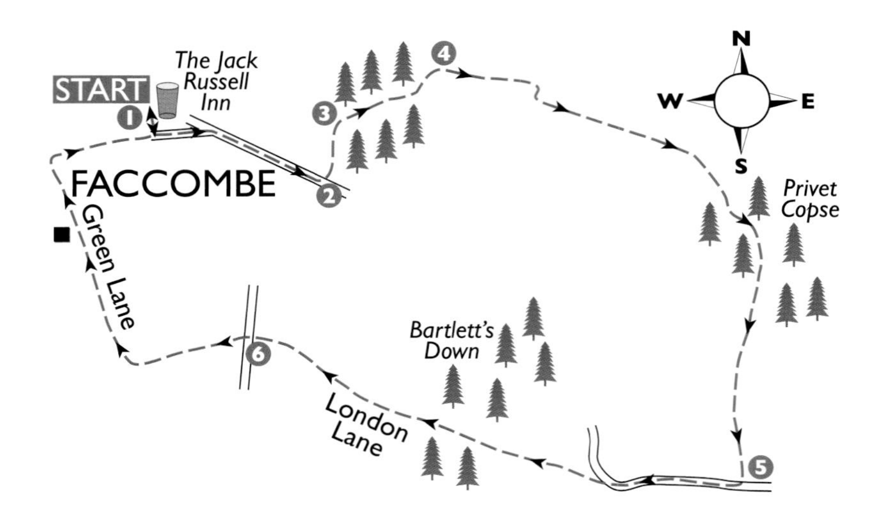

Turn left here through a gap by the gate and walk ahead by the side of the hedge, with the field on your right. At the end of the field, turn right by a waymarker post and follow the grassy path towards woods.

3 Walk through the woods, heading steeply downhill and ignoring all side paths. Head right out of the woods and follow the path to a crossroads, with two small brick and flint farm buildings on either side of the lane on your right.

4 Turn right and walk past the brick farm building on your left, then at the footpath sign just past this, there is a choice of three paths, where you follow the public footpath on the left. Stay on this path, bearing left at a clearing, as it leads you along the valley.

5 Eventually you come to farm gates and a road. Turn right and walk by the side of the road, then as it bends sharply to the right, go straight on to follow the footpath through the woods. This is an ancient track known as **London Lane**. Walk uphill through the woods and stay on this path until you come to a road.

6 Cross the road carefully and walk by the side of metal gates then along a wide grass avenue called **Green Lane**, following the

footpath sign. This path leads you to a T-junction. Turn right to follow the footpath sign, still on Green Lane, until you come to a large, metal barn. Walk with the barn on your left and follow the track to walk by the side of metal gates to the village road, then turn immediately right to return to **The Jack Russell Inn**.

Place of Interest Nearby

Highclere Castle is the ancestral home of the Earls of Carnarvon, although it is better known as the fictional home of the Earl and Countess of Grantham in the TV series ***Downton Abbey***, which was filmed on location at Highclere. Many of the interior rooms, as well as the grounds, will look very familiar from the TV series.

The 5th Earl of Carnarvon financed the archaeological work of Howard Carter, who discovered the tomb of Tutankhamun in the Valley of the Kings in Egypt, in 1922. Carnarvon was present when the tomb was opened, and died a few months later from an infection, starting the story of the 'Curse of Tutankamun', as several other members of the team also died in mysterious circumstances. There is a fascinating Egyptian Exhibition downstairs at the castle. 🌐 highclerecastle.co.uk

Walk 20
SILCHESTER

Distance: 5 miles (8 km)

Map: OS Explorer 159 Reading, Wokingham & Pangbourne.
Grid ref: SU627622

How to get there: Silchester is 5 miles north of Basingstoke, on the Berkshire border. The pub and car park are in the centre of this small village next to the common. **Sat nav:** RG7 2PH.

Parking: Free parking by Silchester Village Hall.

Silchester is a pretty village, dominated by a large common, a rare area of acid heathland that is popular with families and walkers. The pub is by the common and is a lovely spot to sit and watch the world go by. Silchester is also the site of Calleva Atrebatum, a large Roman town managed by English Heritage. The walk explores the city walls and amphitheatre, before heading off to enjoy the surrounding countryside. It's easy walking with lovely views across the pastoral landscape. The land is mainly arable but there are cattle in some of the fields. The farmers have put notices up where there is livestock, giving dog walkers time to put their canine companion on a lead. There is no road walking and you probably won't see anyone once you leave the Roman town, making this a lovely peaceful walk filled with birdsong in the summer.

THE PUB **THE CALLEVA ARMS** is a friendly village pub, popular with walkers and locals. It is a Fuller's pub with a reputation for serving great ale. They also serve classic pub food with the choice of people-watching from the tables outside, or relaxing in the tastefully decorated interior.

🌐 callevaarms.co.uk
☎ 0118 970 0305

The Walk

1 With your back to the pub, cross the road to the car park and take the path at the far end. Pass the stone war memorial on your left and follow the narrow path that leads you through trees to a surfaced track. Cross, then turn left, then right, along an access road. Pass some pretty cottages and stay on this path, ignoring a footpath on your left until you come to a gate. Go through the gate and you are at the western edge of the Roman town of ***Calleva Atrebatum***.

2 Turn left, passing the information board and map of the site, then go through the gate, to follow the walls to the north gate. As you approach the building of **Manor Farm** and the church over on your right, look out for a footpath and turn left here, following the **Brenda Parker Way**, to visit the amphitheatre. At the road, turn right and look out for a gap in the hedge on the other side that takes you to the amphitheatre.

3 When you have finished, retrace your steps back to the road and through the gate to return to the walls. Turn left and continue walking until you come to a gate. Go through the gate, then turn right and go through the gate next to it, to walk past **St Mary the Virgin Church**. Walk through the churchyard to a road.

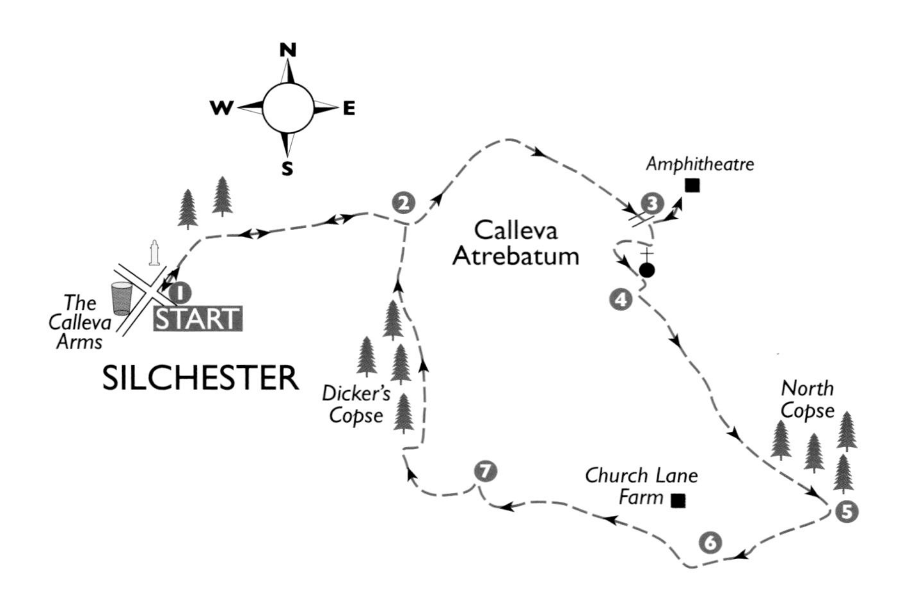

❹ Take the footpath opposite the churchyard, signed Brenda Parker Way, then walk straight across the field, through a copse, then across another field to a large oak tree by a surfaced track. Turn right and follow the track round the corner and to the bottom of the field to a cross track. Go ahead through a metal swing gate and follow the footpath ahead, with the field on your right, and **North Copse** the other side of the fence on your left.

❺ At the other end of the field, don't go through the gate, instead turn right and through a metal kissing gate into another field. Walk ahead to a fingerpost and head diagonally across the field following the footpath. Cross a small area of scrub between two fields, then diagonally across the next field. At the opposite edge of the field, turn right along the footpath. Go through two metal kissing gates and you will see farm buildings ahead.

❻ Cross the track and go through a metal kissing gate to follow a path fenced off from the field. Go through another gate into a large field and continue ahead and through another kissing gate. Walk across the left side of the field to a narrow road.